編者的話

　　「國中教育會考」已經實施了兩年，除了「聽力測驗」以外，其他題型和以前的「基本學力測驗」大同小異。聽力不是只聽幾份試題就可以，要經過大量的聽力測驗才行。所以，我們另外出版三本聽力的書：「國中會考英語聽力進階」和「國中會考英語聽力測驗①②」，聽力一定要練到做新的題目滿分為止。

　　本書收錄歷屆的「國中教育會考英語科試題及詳解」。每一份試題都經過命題老師一再斟酌考量之後，才呈現在考生面前。你了解過去出什麼題目，今年出什麼題目，就知道明年題目會怎麼考。考試的方向和重點，就在這些考題中，同學只要徹底研究這些資料，就能攻克「國中會考」。

　　「劉毅英文」成立四十多年，全國性的考試我們都會做詳解，並且請美國權威教授徹底校對，並製作「勘誤表」，供老師和出題者參考。如「103年國中會考英語科試題」第50題中的 best-selling movie 應改成 most popular movie 或 most successful movie，因為 best-selling（暢銷的）是指商品的銷售，如書或 DVD。再如「104年國中會考英語科試題」第7題：I don't like any one of these three watches. 應改成 I don't like *any* of these three watches. 因為 one 是多餘的。英文實在太難了，只要是中國人寫英文，就難免會出錯。

　　本書編校製作過程嚴謹，但仍恐有疏漏之處，誠望各界先進不吝指正。

劉　毅

105 年國中教育會考英語科試題

閱讀測驗（第 1-41 題，共 41 題）

第一部分：單題（第 1-15 題，共 15 題）

1. Look at the picture. What is the dog doing?
   (A) Biting the man.
   (B) Crossing the street.
   (C) Running after the bus.
   (D) Sitting on the sidewalk.

2. Chris: Which _____ looks better on me?
   Penny: I think purple's better. You look great in purple.
   (A) color　　(B) grade　　(C) shape　　(D) size

3. My cat got excited when it saw the boy _____ the birds.
   (A) catches　(B) catching　(C) to catch　(D) caught

4. Mr. Jackson is a very _____ writer; people of all ages enjoy his stories.
   (A) polite　　(B) popular　　(C) handsome　　(D) honest

5. Carol sounded happy when we talked on the phone; I could feel joy in her _____.
   (A) eyes　　(B) mail　　(C) smile　　(D) voice

6. Mark studies very hard and never _____ classes. He goes to school even when he is sick.
   (A) loses　　(B) misses　　(C) changes　　(D) forgets

7. Have you got anything for Joe _____? He'd be happy to get your gift on his birthday.
   (A) almost   (B) either   (C) soon   (D) yet

8. Susan bought _____ bread in the supermarket, but she did not buy anything to drink.
   (A) many   (B) some   (C) any   (D) one

9. Playing sports at least three times a week _____ good for your health.
   (A) is   (B) are   (C) has   (D) have

10. My parents have different hobbies. One enjoys baking; _____ enjoys taking pictures.
    (A) another   (B) the next   (C) the other   (D) the second

11. My mom told me to take care of _____ in England. She worried that I couldn't eat or sleep well there.
    (A) me   (B) myself   (C) her   (D) herself

12. The paint on the wall is not as _____ as it was ten years ago. It has changed from white to gray.
    (A) bright   (B) heavy   (C) sure   (D) young

13. I told you this road went the wrong way, but you just wouldn't listen. Now we have to _____ and take another road.
    (A) go ahead   (B) move away   (C) pass by   (D) turn back

14. The last five years have not been _____ to Jennie. Her face is covered with lines and she looks much older than she is.

(A) kind　　　　(B) special　　　　(C) real　　　　(D) enough

15. My dog Jimmy loves _____ with a comb. Every time I comb his hair, he will close his eyes and fall asleep.

(A) to brush　　　　　　　(B) brushing

(C) to be brushing　　　　　(D) being brushed

第二部分：題組（第 16-41 題，共 26 題）

（16-17）

> Our Pinky Street, one of the oldest streets in the world, was almost lost to a big fire last night. Most of the old houses on Pinky were burned down. The living history we are proud of is dying. But we should never give up. Pinky is like a parent, always there caring for our town. Now we must do something together to get the old Pinky back. There will be a meeting at 2:00 this Saturday afternoon at Town Office. Anyone who wants to help is welcome. Let's see what we can do.
>
> Adam Bolton, Town Office
>
> March 9

16. What is the reading for?

    (A) Finding out why the old street was on fire.

    (B) Inviting people to do business on the old street.

    (C) Getting people to find ways to save the old street.

    (D) Asking for help for people who got hurt in the fire.

17. Which is NOT used in the reading to talk about the old street?

    (A) A good friend.   (B) The old Pinky.

    (C) A parent.   (D) A living history.

（18-20）

FunGana 2016

No idea where to spend your vacation? If you are a big fan of sun, beach, and water sports, then you must join FunGana 2016!

Over the years, FunGana has taken people to many places in Gana. This year, we are taking you to Piso Island, one of Gana's beautiful islands. Piso Island is <u>adjacent to</u> Wako Island, the biggest island in Gana, so it is only 15 minutes away by boat from Wako Island. The best time to visit? All year around, the weather on Piso Island is just wonderful for a vacation. You can sail out to watch whales, or enjoy one of the best mud springs in the world. We will also show you around the island in a special car, the Cocoon Rider. It's our pleasure to help you enjoy your stay on Piso Island.

Find out more about FunGana 2016 at http://www.fungana 2016.com.gn.

18. What is FunGana 2016 for?
    (A) Studying sea animals in Gana.
    (B) Giving courses in water sports.
    (C) Giving weather reports in Gana.
    (D) Helping people experience Gana.

19. What does the reading say about Piso Island?
    (A) It makes the best cars in Gana.
    (B) It has nice weather in every season.
    (C) It is the most popular island in Gana.
    (D) It has the most mud springs in the world.

20. What does adjacent to mean?
    (A) Like.
    (B) Near.
    (C) Bigger than.
    (D) Warmer than.

（21-22）

Here is the schedule with the notice of the summer school that Tina goes to.

Time \ Day	Mon.	Tues.	Wed.	Thurs.	Fri.
09:30～10:30	English	Computer	English	English	Piano
10:40～11:40	Piano	English	Painting	Dancing	Dancing
13:30～14:30	Tennis	Painting	Tennis	Painting	Computer
14:40～15:40	Baseball	Baseball	Swimming	Basketball	Basketball

◈ NOTICE ◈

✦ The school restaurant is closed during the summer school (7/4~7/31). Please bring your own lunch. If you need to order lunch, please tell your class leader the day before.

✦ Dancing shoes can be borrowed with your summer school card. Please find Mr. Shum in Room 117.

✦ During the third week, the gym will be used for the High School Ball Games. Please go to the playground for the basketball classes of the week.

📖 schedule 課表

21. What do we know from the notice?

　(A) The summer school is three weeks long.

　(B) Students can order lunch from the school restaurant.

　(C) There are basketball classes in the gym every week except the third week.

　(D) Those who need to borrow dancing shoes must tell Mr. Shum the day before.

22. Below is what Tina told her friends about the classes in her summer school schedule.

　　Mr. Reed was really crazy to give us so many new words at one time. Who can possibly remember all of them in a night? In our art class, when Ms. Grant asked us to draw a picture, I just drew a mad me looking at Mr. Reed. But then I totally forgot about Mr. Reed after two hours of PE classes in the afternoon. I was just too tired to think! Luckily, there was no computer class today to make it a really bad day.

Which day was Tina talking about?

(A) Monday.　　　　　　　(B) Tuesday.

(C) Wednesday.　　　　　　(D) Thursday.

（ 23-24 ）

The wind keeps blowing.
The door keeps opening.
Will you be with me, my dear Lucy,
When I look for candy
Down there in the dark, dark kitchen?

The wind keeps crying.
The door keeps shaking.
Will you be with me, my dear Lucy,
When I pick up my toy puppy
Out there on the high, high balcony?

Wish you could always be with me
And make them go away with your Do-Re-Me.
I remember last Halloween
They ran away when you started to sing,
"Dear Tommy, my little king,
Close your eyes and have a sweet dream."

So please stay with me and sing
To stop them kicking the door, riding the wind,
And pulling me down to their house under the ground.
They'll go away if you sing here for me,
In a voice that gets a black cat's hair standing,
The strongest legs shaking, and the window glass breaking.

(ideas from Matthew Sweeney's poem)

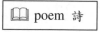 poem 詩

23. Which is most likely true about the speaker in the reading?

📖 likely　可能

   (A) He thinks a black cat is hiding somewhere in the house.

   (B) He feels lonely because he is the only child in his family.

   (C) He is looking for something he left somewhere in the house.

   (D) He is afraid of being by himself when he feels ghosts around.

24. What can we learn about Lucy in the reading?

   (A) She keeps opening the door.

   (B) Her voice makes the speaker feel safe.

   (C) Her candy was hidden in the kitchen.

   (D) She was away from home last Halloween.

（ 25-27 ）

25. What does <u>IT</u> in picture 7 mean?

    (A) Rule 22 is easy to follow.

    (B) Anyone can die at any time.

    (C) Flying airplanes is dangerous.

    (D) The soldier has become crazy.

26. What can we learn from the comics?

    (A) The doctor tried several ways to help the soldier.

    (B) The soldier cared about his life more than his job.

    (C) The soldier went to ask the doctor about Rule 22.

    (D) The use of "catch-22" appeared before Joseph Heller's book.

27. From the comics, which is most likely an example of "catch-22"?

> 📖 likely 可能

    (A) I need to go to hospital, but there are no hospitals near my house.

    (B) I need my key to open the door of my house, but I left my key at school.

    (C) I need some special experience to get this job, but I can't get this kind of experience except from this job.

    (D) I want to go out with Jennifer on New Year's Day, but I'm not sure whether she wants to go out with me that day.

（28-31）

Alec: So, what do you think about <u>it</u>?

Ellie: It's…interesting.

Alec: Oh, no, don't say that.

Ellie: The first thing you should know about Olivia is that she's scared of anything with six legs. I don't think she'll be able to walk past the gate of Buzzing World.

Alec: But she loves butterflies! Well, she loved the photos of butterflies I took last time I was there.

Ellie: Only when they're not moving.

Alec: Fine. I'll just take her somewhere else, and that'd be OK. Right?

Ellie: Umm, you're taking her to Wavelength for dinner?

Alec: What's wrong with that?!

Ellie: I wouldn't say a dead fish is really her idea of a nice dinner, and this restaurant sells seafood…

Alec: Now you're wrong about <u>this one</u>. She loved my mom's fish balls. She had several last time!

Ellie: OK, let's ask someone else. Oh, there's Lori. Hey, Lori, could you look at Alec's plan? He's taking Olivia out.

Lori: Wow! Everything's written down on paper! Hmmm… I thought you wanted her to be your girlfriend.

Alec: I do!

Lori: If you follow this plan, I'm sure it'll be your only date with her.

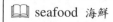
seafood　海鮮

28. What does <u>it</u> in the first line mean?

    (A) The gate of Buzzing World.

    (B) Alec's butterfly photo.

    (C) Alec's plan for his date.

    (D) Anything with six legs.

29. What does <u>this one</u> mean in the dialogue?

    (A) What food Wavelength sells.

    (B) Why Olivia does not like seafood.

    (C) What Alec thinks about Wavelength.

    (D) What food Olivia does not like to eat.

30. What can we learn about Alec?

    (A) He was told that Olivia likes nice surprises.

    (B) He decided to cook Olivia a nice seafood dinner.

    (C) He was happy that Olivia was finally his girlfriend.

    (D) He gave up the idea of taking Olivia to Buzzing World.

31. Emily is a friend of Olivia's. If she agrees with Lori, what would she most likely say to Alec?

    📖 likely 可能

    (A) "This is just what Olivia would want!"

    (B) "You never know what a girl like Olivia would want."

    (C) "Make a different plan or have a date with a different girl!"

    (D) "She never cares what she does on a date; she cares who she has a date with."

（32-34）

Since the first case of "Cow Cold" was reported in Kirk State in June, this killer cold has moved up north faster than we thought it would. By July, almost every part of the country had been attacked by Cow Cold. In only two months, the number of dead cows has risen to 5,000. Though Cow Cold started in the south, the east of the country is the worst hit area. By this week, 80% of the farms in Osten State have reported cases of Cow Cold.

The sale of milk in Osten State has <u>slumped</u> because of Cow Cold. Before Cow Cold, the sale of milk in Osten State was $2.5 million each week; now it is less than $500,000.

Odin State is the only area in the north without cases of Cow Cold. Before we know how to deal with Cow Cold, we can only hope Odin State will be lucky enough not to experience the power of this killer cold.

(Elaine Baker, *City Post*)

📖 case 案例　area 區域

32. What can we learn from the news report?

(A) How to deal with Cow Cold.

(B) Whether people may catch Cow Cold.

(C) How fast Cow Cold has hit the country.

(D) How to find out if cows have Cow Cold.

33. Which map will most likely appear with the above news report?

📖 likely　可能

(A) (B) (C) (D)

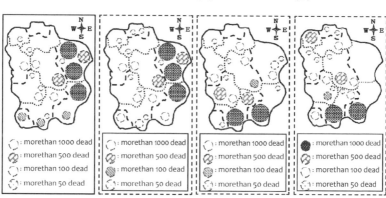

34. If a store's sales keep <u>slump</u>ing, what would the sales chart look like?

📖 likely　可能

(A)

(B)

(C)

(D)

（ 35-38 ）

It was 11 p.m. and Molly walked out of her bakery. She turned and looked at her store one last time. She wanted to remember what it __35__ at the moment. A few hours later, people would come and clean out everything in the store. A young man had bought it. He __36__ it into a flower shop.

Before it was a bakery, this place __37__ a small coffee shop. Molly worked in the shop as a waitress. But taking orders was never Molly's dream; baking was. When she knew her boss planned to sell the shop, she borrowed money and bought it.

Her bakery had been open for thirty years. Thirty very wonderful years. However, it would all come to an end tonight. Molly __38__ the bakery to be a family business. But her daughter was never interested in baking. Molly did not want her business in a stranger's hands, so after some serious thinking, she decided to close it.

"Goodbye, my dear old friend," Molly looked at the store, whispering.

📖 whisper 低語

35. (A) had looked like   (B) looked like
    (C) would look like   (D) has looked like

36. (A) had changed   (B) changed
    (C) was going to change   (D) has changed

37. (A) used to be　　　　　　(B) would be
　　(C) has been　　　　　　 (D) is

38. (A) had wanted　　　　　　(B) has wanted
　　(C) would want　　　　　 (D) will want

（39-41）

What does the word family mean to you? An American study in 2006 showed that people today ___39___. Over 99% of the people who were interviewed agree that a husband, a wife, and a child are a family. At the same time, 94% see a parent with a child as a family, 91% say a husband and a wife, without children, are a family, and 81% think a man and a woman, with a child, but not married, are a family too.

The study also found that ___40___ is very important in the modern thinking on family. Though 81% think a man and a woman, not married, with a child, are a family, the percentage (%) drops to 40% if the couple doesn't have a child. This is also true with same-sex couples. About 60% see two men, or two women, with a child, as a family, but only 32% think so when the couple doesn't have a child.

In the study, those who see two men or two women that live together as a family often find it OK for same-sex couples to get married.   41 . However, not everyone opens their arms to same-sex couples: the study said 30% have no problem seeing pets as part of one's family, but they do not think a same-sex couple is a family.

📖 couple 伴侶　same-sex 同性

39. (A) think differently about when to start a family
    (B) do not find family as important as their parents did
    (C) want many different things when they start a family
    (D) have several different ideas about what makes a family

40. (A) whether people are married or not
    (B) whether people have a child or not
    (C) whether people live together or not
    (D) whether people love each other or not

41. (A) This is not surprising
    (B) This is not possible everywhere
    (C) It is no good news for everyone
    (D) It cannot be this way for very long

聽力測驗（第 1-21 題，共 21 題）

第一部分：辨識句意（第 1-3 題，共 3 題）

作答說明： 第 1-3 題每題有三張圖片，請依據所聽到的內容，選出
符合描述的圖片，每題播放兩次。

示例題：你會看到

(A)　　　　　　　(B)　　　　　　　(C)

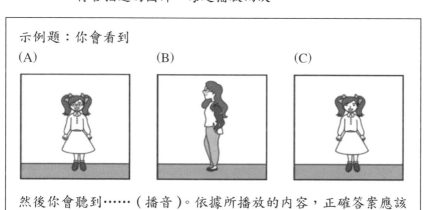

然後你會聽到……（播音）。依據所播放的內容，正確答案應該
選 A，請將答案卡該題「Ⓐ」的地方塗黑、塗滿，即：● Ⓑ Ⓒ

1. (A)　　　　　　　(B)　　　　　　　(C)

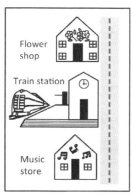
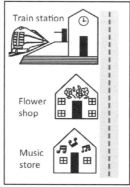

2. (A)　　　　　　　(B)　　　　　　　(C)

3. (A)　　　　　　　(B)　　　　　　　(C)

第二部分：基本問答（第 4-10 題，共 7 題）

作答說明：　第 4-10 題每題均有三個選項，請依據所聽到的內容，選
　　　　　　出一個最適合的回應，每題播放兩次。

示例題：你會看到

(A) She is talking to the teacher.

(B) She is a student in my class.

(C) She is wearing a beautiful dress.

然後你會聽到……（播音）。依據所播放的內容，正確答案應該
選 B，請將答案卡該題「Ⓑ」的地方塗黑、塗滿，即：Ⓐ ● Ⓒ

4. (A) It's 12:30.
   (B) It's 2345-6789.
   (C) It's May 26, 1998.

5. (A) So did I.
   (B) Thanks for telling me.
   (C) No. Any big news?

6. (A) Get ready.
   (B) Good job.
   (C) No problem.

7. (A) I know! You cooked well.
   (B) Yes, I knew you'd like it.
   (C) When did you order the
       food?

8. (A) Oh, thank you.
   (B) Oh, excuse me.
   (C) Oh, you're lucky.

9. (A) After school.
   (B) At the park.
   (C) In the refrigerator.

10. (A) I can't wait.
    (B) It didn't take long.
    (C) That's too slow.

第三部分：言談理解（第 11-21 題，共 11 題）

作答說明： 第 11-21 題每題均有三個選項，請依據所聽到的內容，
          選出一個最適合的答案，每題播放兩次。

示例題：你會看到

(A) 9:50.　　(B) 10:00.　　(C) 10:10.

然後你會聽到……（播音）。依據所播放的內容，正確答案應該
選 B，請將答案卡該題「Ⓑ」的地方塗黑、塗滿，即：Ⓐ ● Ⓒ

---

11. (A) Science.
    (B) Sports.
    (C) Reading.

12. (A) A taxi driver.
    (B) A shopkeeper.
    (C) A police officer.

13. (A) The man's shoes.
    (B) The trash can.
    (C) Tom's noodles.

14. (A) Ted's mother.
    (B) Ted's sister.
    (C) Ted's friend.

15. (A) Cooking food.
    (B) Making a shopping list.
    (C) Buying dinner for the man.

16. (A) A library.
    (B) A theater.
    (C) A restaurant.

17. (A) Having a job interview.
    (B) Ordering their food.
    (C) Talking about some news.

18. (A) She did not know the plan had been changed.
    (B) She is waiting for the bus to the museum.
    (C) She made a mistake about where to meet.

19. (A) She feels lonely at school.
    (B) She's not interested in drawing pictures.
    (C) She's just started going to a new school.

20. (A) It was boring.
    (B) It was exciting.
    (C) It was serious.

21. (A) For her book.
    (B) For her movie.
    (C) For her news report.

105年國中教育會考英語科試題詳解

閱讀測驗（第 1-41 題，共 41 題）

第一部分：單題（第 1-15 題，共 15 題）

1.（**B**）看看這張圖片。那隻狗正在做什麼？

(A) 咬那個男人。

(B) <u>過馬路。</u>

(C) 追公車。

(D) 坐在人行道上。

* bite〔baɪt〕*v.* 咬　　cross〔krɔs〕*v.* 橫越
run after 追趕　　sidewalk〔'saɪd,wɔk〕*n.* 人行道

2.（**A**）克里斯：我穿哪個<u>顏色</u>比較好看？

潘　妮：我認為紫色比較好。你穿紫色很好看。

(A) ***color***〔'kʌlɚ〕*n.* 顏色

(B) grade〔gred〕*n.* 成績

(C) shape〔ʃep〕*n.* 形狀

(D) size〔saɪz〕*n.* 尺寸；大小

* look〔lʊk〕*v.* 看起來　　purple〔'pɝpḷ〕*n.* 紫色
great〔gret〕*adj.* 很棒的　　in〔ɪn〕*prep.* 穿著

3.（**B**）我的貓看到那個小男孩<u>在捉鳥</u>時，變得很興奮。

saw 是感官動詞 see（看）的過去式，接受詞後，接原形動
詞或現在分詞表「主動」，接過去分詞表「被動」，依句意，
選 (B) ***catching***。　　catch〔kætʃ〕*v.* 捕捉

* excited〔ɪk'saɪtɪd〕*adj.* 興奮的

4.（**B**）傑克森先生是位非常<u>受歡迎的</u>作家；所有的人，不分年齡，都
喜歡他的故事。

(A) polite〔pə'laɪt〕*adj.* 有禮貌的

(B) ***popular***〔'pɑpjəlɚ〕*adj.* 受歡迎的

(C) handsome〔ˈhænsəm〕adj. 英俊的

(D) honest〔ˈɑnɪst〕adj. 誠實的

＊writer〔ˈraɪtə〕n. 作家　　age〔edʒ〕n. 年齡

of all ages 所有不同年齡的　　enjoy〔ɪnˈdʒɔɪ〕v. 喜歡；享受

5.(**D**) 當我們在講電話時，卡蘿聽起來很高興；我可以在她的聲音裡感受到喜悅。

(A) eyes〔aɪz〕n. pl. 眼睛　　(B) mail〔mel〕n. 郵件

(C) smile〔smaɪl〕n. 微笑　　(D) **voice**〔vɔɪs〕n. 聲音

＊sound〔saʊnd〕v. 聽起來　　**talk on the phone** 講電話

feel〔fil〕v. 感受到　　joy〔dʒɔɪ〕n. 喜悅

6.(**B**) 馬克非常用功，從未錯過任何一堂課。他甚至在生病時也去上學。

(A) lose〔luz〕v. 失去　　(B) **miss**〔mɪs〕v. 錯過

(C) change〔tʃendʒ〕v. 改變　(D) forget〔fəˈgɛt〕v. 忘記

＊**study hard** 用功讀書　　class〔klæs〕n. 課

sick〔sɪk〕adj. 生病的

7.(**D**) 你已經有買任何東西給喬了嗎？他在生日時收到你的禮物，一定會很高興。

(A) almost〔ˈɔlˌmost〕adv. 幾乎

(B) either〔ˈiðə〕adv. 也（不）

(C) soon〔sun〕adv. 很快；不久

(D) **yet**〔jɛt〕adv.【用於疑問句】已經

＊get〔gɛt〕v. 買；得到　　gift〔gɪft〕n. 禮物

8.(**B**) 蘇珊在超市買了一些麵包，但是她並沒有買任何飲料。

bread（麵包）是不可數名詞，所以 (A) many 和 (D) one 用法不合，(C) any（任何的）則是用於疑問句或否定句，在此也不合，故選 (B) **some**（一些）。

＊bread〔brɛd〕n. 麵包

supermarket〔ˈsupəˌmɑrkɪt〕n. 超級市場

9. (**A**) 一週至少運動三次對健康有益。

　　動名詞片語 Playing…week 當主詞，視爲單數，要用
　　單數動詞，故本題選 (A) *is*。

　　* sport〔sport〕*n.* 運動

10. (**C**) 我父母親的嗜好不同。一個喜歡烘焙；另一個喜歡拍照。

　　父母親有兩人，表示「(二者中的)另一個」，代名詞用
　　the other，故選 (C)。

　　* hobby〔'hɑbɪ〕*n.* 嗜好　　bake〔bek〕*v.* 烘焙
　　take pictures 拍照

11. (**B**) 我媽媽告訴我在英國要照顧自己。她擔心我在那裡吃不好、
睡不好。

　　依句意是「照顧我自己」，主詞和受詞爲同一人，受詞用
　　反身代名詞，選 (B) *myself*。

　　* *take care of* 照顧　　England〔'ɪŋglənd〕*n.* 英國
　　worry〔'wɝɪ〕*v.* 擔心

12. (**A**) 牆壁上的油漆不像十年前那麼亮，已經從白色變成灰色。

　　(A) *bright*〔braɪt〕*adj.* 明亮的
　　(B) heavy〔'hɛvɪ〕*adj.* 重的
　　(C) sure〔ʃur〕*adj.* 確定的
　　(D) young〔jʌŋ〕*adj.* 年輕的
　　* paint〔pent〕*n.* 油漆　　gray〔gre〕*adj.* 灰色的

13. (**D**) 我告訴過你這條路的方向錯誤，但你就是不聽。現在我們必須
調頭回去，走另外一條路。

　　(A) go ahead　進行
　　(B) move away　移開；挪開
　　(C) pass by　經過；(時間)過去
　　(D) *turn back*　返回

14.(**A**) 過去五年對吉妮而言並不<u>輕鬆</u>。她的臉上增添了皺紋,她看起來
比實際年齡老多了。

(A) **kind** 〔 kaɪnd 〕 *adj.* 仁慈的;寬容的

(B) special 〔 ˈspɛʃəl 〕 *adj.* 特別的

(C) real 〔 ˈriəl 〕 *adj.* 真正的

(D) enough 〔 əˈnʌf 〕 *adj.* 足夠的

* last 〔 læst 〕 *adj.* 過去的　　　cover 〔 ˈkʌvɚ 〕 *v.* 覆蓋
line 〔 laɪn 〕 *n.* 線條;皺紋

15.(**D**) 我的狗吉米喜歡用梳子<u>梳毛</u>。每次我幫牠梳毛,牠就會閉上眼
睛睡著。

love 後面可以接動名詞和不定詞,而小狗應是「被梳理」,
要用被動,故本題選 (D) **being brushed**。

brush 〔 brʌʃ 〕 *v.* 刷

* comb 〔 kom 〕 *n.* 梳子　 *v.* 梳理　　　***fall asleep*** 睡著

第二部分:題組（第 16-41 題,共 26 題）

（16~17）

> 我們的桃紅街,是世界上最古老的街之一,昨晚幾乎滅
> 於一場大火。大部分在桃紅街上的老房子都被燒毀。我們引
> 以為傲的活歷史瀕臨死亡。但是我們絕不該放棄。桃紅街像
> 是雙親之一,總是在那裡照顧我們的城鎮。現在我們必須一
> 起做些事來讓老桃紅復原。這個星期六下午兩點在鎮公所會
> 有一場會議。任何想要幫忙的人都很歡迎。讓我們來看看我
> 們能做什麼。
>
> 　　　　　　　　　　　　　　　　亞當‧波頓,鎮公所
> 　　　　　　　　　　　　　　　　三月九日

【註釋】

pinky〔'pɪŋkɪ〕*adj.* 桃紅色的　　street〔strit〕*n.* 街道

old〔old〕*adj.* 古老的　　world〔wɜld〕*n.* 世界

almost〔'ɔl,most〕*adv.* 幾乎；差不多　　lose〔luz〕*v.* 輸；敗

fire〔faɪr〕*n.* 火災　　burn〔bɜn〕*v.* 燃燒

living〔'lɪvɪŋ〕*adj.* 活的　　history〔'hɪstrɪ〕*n.* 歷史

proud〔praʊd〕*adj.* 驕傲的　　***be proud of*** 以…感到光榮

dying〔'daɪɪŋ〕*adj.* 垂死的；瀕死的　　***give up*** 放棄

parent〔'pɛrənt〕*n.* 雙親之一　　***care for*** 照顧

town〔taʊn〕*n.* 城鎮　　together〔tə'gɛðɚ〕*adv.* 一起

get sth. back 復原；恢復　　meeting〔'mitɪŋ〕*n.* 會議

office〔'ɔfɪs〕*n.* …處；…所

welcome〔'wɛlkəm〕*adj.* 受歡迎的

Let's … 讓我們來… (= *Let us*…)

16. (**C**) 本文是爲了什麼？

(A) 找出爲什麼老街會失火。

(B) 邀請人們在老街上做生意。

(C) 聚集人們尋找拯救老街的方法。

(D) 爲在火災中受傷的人們請求援助。

　*　**find out** 找出　　**on fire** 著火

　　invite〔ɪn'vaɪt〕*v.* 邀請　　find〔faɪnd〕*v.* 尋找

　　way〔we〕*n.* 方法　　save〔sev〕*v.* 拯救

　　ask〔æsk〕*v.* 請求　　hurt〔hɜt〕*v.* 使受傷

17. (**A**) 何者並未在本文中被用來談論老街？

(A) 好朋友。

(B) 老桃紅。

(C) 雙親之一。

(D) 活歷史。

　*　use〔juz〕*v.* 使用　　***talk about*** 談論；談到

（18～20）

2016 樂趣迦拿

　　不知道要去哪裡渡假嗎？如果你是太陽、海灘和水上運動的忠實粉絲，那麼你必須加入 2016 樂趣迦拿！

　　多年來，樂趣迦拿已經帶人們到迦拿的許多地方。今年，我們帶你去迦拿的美麗島嶼之一的披索島。披索島<u>毗鄰</u>迦拿的最大島哇寇島，所以它距離哇寇島只要十五分鐘的船程。最佳造訪時間？整年下來，披索島的天氣對假期來說是再適合不過了。你可以航行出海賞鯨，或者享受全世界最好之一的泥泉。我們也會用特殊車輛，<u>蠶繭</u>騎手，帶你到島上到處看看。協助你享受待在披索島是我們的榮幸。

　　在 <u>http://www.fungana2016.com.gn</u> 這個網站找出更多關於 2016 樂趣迦拿的資訊。

【註釋】

idea〔aɪˈdiə〕*n.* 了解；認識　　***no idea*** 不知道

spend〔spɛnd〕*v.* 花（時間）　　vacation〔veˈkeʃən〕*n.* 假期

fan〔fæn〕*n.* 愛好者　　sport〔sport〕*n.* 運動

join〔dʒɔɪn〕*v.* 加入　　place〔ples〕*n.* 地點

island〔ˈaɪlənd〕*n.* 島嶼

adjacent〔əˈdʒesn̩t〕*adj.* 毗鄰的；鄰近的

visit〔ˈvɪzɪt〕*v.* 造訪　　***all year round*** 一整年；全年

weather〔ˈwɛðɚ〕*n.* 天氣　　sail〔sel〕*v.* 航行

whale〔hwel〕*n.* 鯨魚　　mud〔mʌd〕*n.* 泥巴

spring〔sprɪŋ〕*n.* 泉　　show〔ʃo〕*v.* 引導；帶領

special〔ˈspɛʃəl〕*adj.* 特殊的　　cocoon〔kəˈkun〕*n.*（蠶）繭

pleasure〔ˈplɛʒɚ〕*n.* 榮幸　　stay〔ste〕*n.* 停留

18. (**D**) 2016 樂趣迦拿是什麼？

　　(A) 研究在迦拿的海洋動物。

　　(B) 提供水上運動的課程。

　　(C) 提供在迦拿的天氣報告。

　　(D) 協助人們體驗迦拿。

　　* study〔'stʌdɪ〕*v.* 研究　　animal〔'ænəml̩〕*n.* 動物

　　course〔kors〕*n.* 課程　　report〔rɪ'port〕*n.* 報告

　　experience〔ɪk'spɪrɪəns〕*v.* 體驗

19. (**B**) 關於披索島，本文說了什麼？

　　(A) 它在迦拿製造最好的車。

　　(B) 它在每個季節都有很好的天氣。

　　(C) 它是迦拿最受歡迎的島嶼。

　　(D) 它有全世界最多的泥泉。

　　* season〔'sizn̩〕*n.* 季節　　popular〔'pɑpjələ〕*adj.* 受歡迎的

20. (**B**) adjacent to 是什麼意思？

　　(A) 像。　　　　　　　　(B) 靠近。

　　(C) 還要大。　　　　　　(D) 還要溫暖。

　　* like〔laɪk〕*prep.* 像　　warm〔wɔrm〕*adj.* 溫暖的

（21～22）

這是蒂娜去的暑期學校的課表和通知。

星期 時間	星期一	星期二	星期三	星期四	星期五
09:30～10:30	英文	電腦	英文	英文	鋼琴
10:40～11:40	鋼琴	英文	繪畫	舞蹈	舞蹈
13:30～14:30	網球	繪畫	網球	繪畫	電腦
14:40～15:40	棒球	棒球	游泳	籃球	籃球

◈ **通知** ◈

↴ 在暑期學校期間（7/4～7/31），學校餐廳關閉。請帶自己的午餐。如果你需要訂午餐，請在前一天告訴你的班長。

↴ 舞鞋可用暑期學校卡借。請找 117 教室的沈先生。

↴ 第三週期間，體育館會作中學球類比賽使用。當週的籃球課請到運動場。

【註釋】

schedule〔'skɛdʒul〕*n.* 時間表；課表　　notice〔'notɪs〕*n.* 通知
summer school 暑期講習會；暑期學校
closed〔klozd〕*adj.* 關閉的　　bring〔brɪŋ〕*v.* 攜帶
own〔on〕*adj.* 自己的　　order〔'ɔrdɚ〕*v.* 訂購
leader〔'lidɚ〕*n.* 領導者　　borrow〔'baro〕*v.* 借
game〔gem〕*n.* 比賽　　playground〔'ple,graʊnd〕*n.* 運動場

21. (**C**) 從這則通知，我們知道什麼？

　　(A) 暑期學校為期三週。
　　(B) 學生可以向學校餐廳訂午餐。
　　(C) 除了第三週，每週在體育館都有籃球課。
　　(D) 凡是需要借舞鞋的人，必須在前一天告訴沈先生。

　　* know〔no〕*v.* 知道　　except〔ɪk'sɛpt〕*prep.* 除了…以外

22. (**C**) 以下是蒂娜告訴她朋友關於暑期學校課表內的課。

　　　瑞得先生真的很瘋狂，想一次給我們許多新單字。有誰可以一個晚上記住所有的字？在我們美術課時，葛蘭特女士要我們畫一張圖，我畫了一個憤怒的我盯著瑞得先生。但是我在下午的兩個小時的體育課後，完全忘掉瑞得先生。我只是累得無法思考！幸好，今天沒有會讓一天真的很不順的電腦課。

蒂娜在說哪一天？

(A) 星期一。　　　　　　(B) 星期二。

(C) 星期三。　　　　　　(D) 星期四。

* crazy〔'krezɪ〕*adj.* 瘋狂的
　 possibly〔'pɑsəblɪ〕*adv.* 可能
　 remember〔rɪ'mɛmbɚ〕*v.* 記住
　 totally〔'totl̩ɪ〕*adv.* 完全地　　***PE class*** 體育課
　 luckily〔'lʌkɪlɪ〕*adv.* 幸好

（23～24）

風一直吹。

門一直打開。

妳會陪著我嗎，我親愛的露西，

當我尋找糖果的時候，

到下面那很黑、很黑的廚房？

風一直呼嘯。

門一直搖動。

妳會陪著我嗎，我親愛的露西，

當我拿起我的小狗玩具，

在那高高的陽台上？

希望妳能總是陪著我

並用妳的歌聲讓它們離開。

我記得去年萬聖節

當妳一開始唱歌，它們就離開了

「親愛的湯米，我的小國王，

閉上你的眼睛，然後做個美夢。」

所以請妳陪著我並唱歌

去阻止它們踢門,乘著風,

並把我拖到它們地底下的房子。

如果妳在這裡為我歌唱,它們就會離開,

用妳的聲音,那會使黑貓的皮毛豎起,

最強壯的腿顫抖,和窗戶的玻璃破裂。

(點子來自馬修・斯威尼的詩)

【註釋】

wind〔wɪnd〕*n.* 風　　***keep + V-ing*** 一直;持續

blow〔blo〕*v.* 吹　　dear〔dɪr〕*adj.* 親愛的

Lucy〔'lusɪ〕*n.*(女子名)露西

look for 尋找　　candy〔'kændɪ〕*n.* 糖果

dark〔dɑrk〕*adj.* 黑暗的;漆黑的　　kitchen〔'kɪtʃɪn〕*n.* 廚房

cry〔kraɪ〕*v.* 喊叫;(風)呼嘯

shake〔ʃek〕*v.* 搖動;搖晃;顫抖

pick up 拿起;拾起　　toy〔tɔɪ〕*n.* 玩具　*adj.* 玩具的

puppy〔'pʌpɪ〕*n.* 小狗　　***out there*** 在外面

balcony〔'bælkənɪ〕*n.* 陽台　　wish〔wɪʃ〕*v.* 希望

always〔'ɔlwɪz〕*adv.* 一直;總是　　***go away*** 離開

Do-Re-Me 音樂;歌聲　　remember〔rɪ'mɛmbɚ〕*v.* 記得

last〔læst〕*adj.* 上一個的;去年的

Halloween〔ˌhælo'in〕*n.* 萬聖節　　***run away*** 跑走

sing〔sɪŋ〕*v.* 唱歌　　Tommy〔'tɑmɪ〕*n.* 湯米

king〔kɪŋ〕*n.* 國王　　close〔kloz〕*v.* 關上;閉上

sweet〔swit〕*adj.* 甜美的;美好的　　dream〔drim〕*n.* 夢

stay with 和…待在一起;陪伴

stop〔stɑp〕*v.* 使停止;阻止　　kick〔kɪk〕*v.* 踢

ride〔raɪd〕*v.* 騎著;駕馭;乘(風)

pull〔pʊl〕*v.* 拉;拖

ground〔graʊnd〕*n.* 地面　　voice〔vɔɪs〕*n.*（人的）聲音
get〔gɛt〕*v.* 使…成為（某狀態）　　black〔blæk〕*adj.* 黑色的
hair〔hɛr〕*n.* 毛髮；（動物的）體毛
stand〔stænd〕*v.* 站立；豎起　　window〔'wɪndo〕*n.* 窗戶
glass〔glæs〕*n.* 玻璃　　break〔brek〕*v.* 破裂
idea〔aɪ'diə〕*n.* 想法；點子　　Matthew〔'mæθju〕*n.* 馬修
Sweeney〔'swinɪ〕*n.* 斯威尼　　poem〔'po·ɪm〕*n.* 詩

23. (**D**) 關於本文的說話者，哪一項最可能為真？
　　(A) 他覺得黑貓躲在房子的某個地方。
　　(B) 他覺得孤單，因為他是家裡的獨子。
　　(C) 他在尋找他在房子裡遺留的東西。
　　(D) 他害怕獨自一人，當他覺得周圍有鬼的時候。

　　* likely〔'laɪklɪ〕*adj.* 可能的
　　　speaker〔'spikɚ〕*n.* 說話者
　　　hide〔haɪd〕*v.* 躲藏
　　　somewhere〔'sʌm,hwɛr〕*adv.* 在某處
　　　lonely〔'lonlɪ〕*adj.* 孤單的　　*only child* 獨生子（女）
　　　left〔lɛft〕*v.* 遺留【leave 的過去式】
　　　be afraid of 害怕　　*by oneself* 獨自地
　　　ghost〔gost〕*n.* 鬼
　　　around〔ə'raʊnd〕*adv.* 在周圍

24. (**B**) 關於文中的露西，我們可以知道什麼？
　　(A) 她一直開門。
　　(B) 她的聲音使說話者感到安全。
　　(C) 她的糖果被藏在廚房。
　　(D) 她去年萬聖節離家。

　　* learn〔lɜn〕*v.* 知道　　safe〔sef〕*adj.* 安全的
　　　hidden〔'hɪdn̩〕*v.* 隱藏【hide 的過去分詞】
　　　be away from 離開

（25～27）

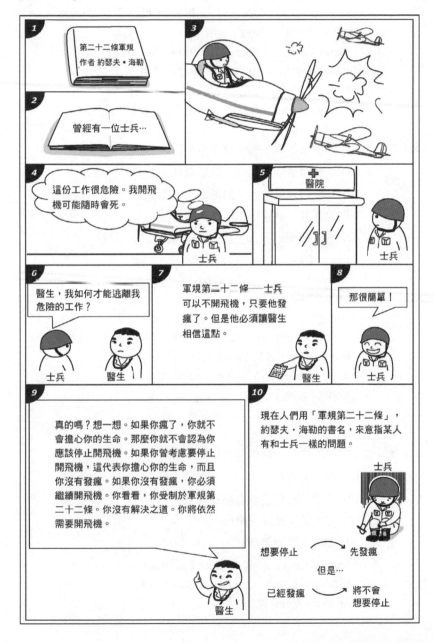

【註釋】

Catch-22 第二十二條軍規【長篇小說，作者是約瑟夫・海勒，這條軍規
規定，只有瘋了的人才可以不出任務，只要由本人親自提出申請，就可
以不出任務】；無可奈何的矛盾；進退兩難的情況(= *dilemma* 〔 dəˈlɛmə 〕)

Joseph 〔ˈdʒozəf〕 *n.* 約瑟夫　　Heller 〔ˈhɛlə〕 *n.* 海勒

there + be 有~　　soldier 〔ˈsoldʒə〕 *n.* 軍人；士兵

job 〔dʒab〕 *n.* 工作　　dangerous 〔ˈdendʒərəs〕 *adj.* 危險的

die 〔daɪ〕 *v.* 死亡；喪生　　*any time* 任何時候；隨時

fly 〔flaɪ〕 *v.* 飛行；開（飛機）　　hospital 〔ˈhɑspɪtl̩〕 *n.* 醫院

doctor 〔ˈdɑktə〕 *n.* 醫生　　*get out of* 擺脫；逃避

rule 〔rul〕 *n.* 規則　　airplane 〔ˈɛrˌplen〕 *n.* 飛機

only if 只有(= *as long as*)　　crazy 〔ˈkrezɪ〕 *adj.* 瘋狂的；發瘋的

have to V. 必須~　　make 〔mek〕 *v.* 使

believe 〔bɪˈliv〕 *v.* 相信　　easy 〔ˈizɪ〕 *adj.* 簡單的；容易的

think about 考慮；想想　　*worry about* 擔心

then 〔ðɛn〕 *adv.* 那麼；然後　　stop 〔stɑp〕 *v.* 停止

ever 〔ˈɛvə〕 *adv.* 曾經　　mean 〔min〕 *v.* 意思是

life 〔laɪf〕 *n.* 生命　　*you see* 你看；你知道的

caught 〔kɔt〕 *v.* 抓住；使捲入【catch 的過去分詞】

be caught 處於（困境）；受制於　　*way out* 出口；解決方法

problem 〔ˈprɑbləm〕 *n.* 問題　　first 〔fɜst〕 *adv.* 首先

already 〔ɔlˈrɛdɪ〕 *adv.* 已經　　got 〔gɑt〕 *v.* 變得【get 的過去式】

25. (**D**) 圖片七的 <u>IT</u> 是什麼意思？

　　(A) 第二十二條軍規很容易遵守。

　　(B) 任何人隨時都可能喪生。

　　(C) 開飛機很危險。

　　(D) <u>士兵已經發瘋。</u>

　　＊ follow 〔ˈfɑlo〕 *v.* 遵守　　*at any time* 在任何時候；隨時

26. (**B**) 從這些連環漫畫，我們可以知道什麼？

　　(A) 醫生嘗試好幾個方法來幫助士兵。

　　(B) <u>士兵關心他的生命勝過他的工作。</u>

(C) 士兵去問醫生關於第二十二條軍規。

(D)「第二十二條軍規」的用法出現在約瑟夫‧海勒的書之前。

* learn〔lɝn〕v. 知道　　comics〔'kɑmɪks〕n. pl. 連環漫畫
  several〔'sɛvərəl〕adj. 幾個的　　way〔we〕n. 方法
  care about 關心　　use〔jus〕n. 使用；用法
  appear〔ə'pɪr〕v. 出現

27.(**C**) 從連環漫畫來看，哪一個最可能是「第二十二條軍規」的例子？

(A) 我需要去醫院，但是在我家附近沒有醫院。

(B) 我需要鑰匙開我家的門，但是我把鑰匙遺留在學校。

(C) <u>我需要一些特別的經驗來得到這份工作，但是除了從這一份工作之外，我無法得到這類的經驗。</u>

(D) 我想要和珍妮佛在元旦一起出去，但是我不確定她那一天是否想要和我一起出去。

* from〔trɑm〕prep. 從…來看　　likely〔'laɪklɪ〕adv. 可能
  example〔ɪg'zæmpl̩〕n. 例子
  near〔nɪr〕prep. 在…的附近　　key〔ki〕n. 鑰匙
  special〔'spɛʃəl〕adj. 特別的
  experience〔ɪk'spɪrɪəns〕n. 經驗　　get〔gɛt〕v. 得到
  kind〔kaɪnd〕n. 種類；類型
  except〔ɪk'sɛpt〕prep. 除了…以外
  Jennifer〔'dʒɛnəfɚ〕n. 珍妮佛　　***New Year's Day*** 元旦
  sure〔ʃʊr〕adj. 確定的　　whether〔'hwɛðɚ〕conj. 是否

(28~31)

艾力克：所以，你覺得它怎麼樣？

艾　莉：它很⋯有趣。

艾力克：喔，不，不要這樣說。

艾　莉：你應該要知道奧莉維亞的第一件事是，她害怕任何有六條腿的東西。我不認為她能夠走過嗡嗡世界的大門。

艾力克：但是她愛蝴蝶！嗯，她愛我上一次在那裡照的蝴蝶的
　　　　照片。

艾　莉：只有當牠們不動時。

艾力克：好。我就帶她去別的地方，那這樣應該可以了，對吧？

艾　莉：嗯，你要帶她去波長吃晚餐？

艾力克：這怎麼了嗎？！

艾　莉：我不會說一條死魚是她真正對於一頓好晚餐的構想，
　　　　而且這家餐廳是賣海鮮的…

艾力克：現在<u>這一點</u>妳就錯了。她愛我媽媽的魚丸。她上次還
　　　　吃了好幾顆！

艾　莉：好，那我們來問問其他人。喔，蘿莉在那邊。嘿，蘿
　　　　莉，妳可以看一下艾力克的計畫嗎？他要約奧莉維亞
　　　　出去。

蘿　莉：哇！一切都寫在紙上！嗯…我認為你是想讓她成為你
　　　　的女朋友。

艾力克：我是想啊！

艾　莉：如果按照這個計劃，我敢肯定這將是你與她的唯一約
　　　　會。

【註釋】

think about 想；考慮　　interesting〔ˋɪntərɪstɪŋ〕*adj.* 有趣的
the first thing 第一件事；首先
scare〔skɛr〕*v.* 驚嚇；使恐懼
be scared of 害怕　　leg〔lɛg〕*n.* 腿；足

be able to V. 能夠…　　past〔pæst〕*prep.* 通過；經過
gate〔get〕*n.* 大門　　buzzing〔'bʌzɪŋ〕*n.* 嗡嗡聲
butterfly〔'bʌtə,flaɪ〕*n.* 蝴蝶　　**take photos** 照相
last time 上次　　move〔muv〕*v.* 移動
somewhere〔'sʌm,hwɛr〕*adv.* 在某處；到某處
else〔ɛls〕*adv.* 另外　　wavelength〔'wev,lɛŋθ〕*n.* 波長
What's wrong with...?　…怎麼了？
dead〔dɛd〕*adj.* 死的；無生命的　　idea〔aɪ'diə〕*n.* 想法；概念
restaurant〔'rɛstərənt〕*n.* 餐館　　sell〔sɛl〕*v.* 賣
seafood〔'si,fud〕*n.* 海鮮　　several〔'sɛvərəl〕*adj.* 數個的
look at 看　　plan〔plen〕*n.* 計畫　　**write down** 寫下
girlfriend〔'gɜl,frɛnd〕*n.* 女朋友
sure〔ʃur〕*adj.* 確信的　　date〔det〕*n.* 約會

28.(**C**) 在第一行的 <u>it</u> 是什麼意思？

　　(A) 嗡嗡世界的大門。　　　　(B) 艾力克的蝴蝶照片。

　　(C) <u>艾力克為他的約會所訂的計畫。</u>

　　(D) 任何有六條腿的東西。

29.(**D**) 在對話中的 <u>this one</u> 是什麼意思？

　　(A) 波長賣什麼樣的食物。

　　(B) 奧莉維亞為什麼不喜歡海鮮。

　　(C) 艾力克對波長的看法。

　　(D) <u>奧莉維亞不喜歡吃什麼食物。</u>

　　* dialogue〔'daɪə,lɔg〕*n.* 對話

30.(**D**) 關於艾力克，我們可以得知什麼？

　　(A) 他被告知奧莉維亞喜歡不錯的驚喜。

　　(B) 他決定為奧莉維亞下廚煮一頓不錯的海鮮晚餐。

　　(C) 他很高興奧莉維亞終於是他的女朋友了。

　　(D) <u>他放棄了帶奧莉維亞去嗡嗡世界的想法。</u>

　　* finally〔'faɪnlɪ〕*adv.* 最後；終於　　**give up** 放棄

31.（**C**）愛蜜莉是奧莉維亞的朋友。如果她同意蘿莉所說的，那她最有可能會對艾力克說什麼？

(A)「這正是奧莉維亞想要的！」

(B)「你絕對不會知道像奧莉維亞這樣的女孩想要什麼。」

(C) <u>「做一個不同的計劃，或是和不同的女孩約會！」</u>

(D)「她從不在乎她在一場約會中做什麼；她在乎的是她跟誰約會。」

＊ ***agree with*** 同意　　different〔ˋdɪfərənt〕*adj.* 不同的
care〔kɛr〕*v.* 在乎；介意

（32～34）

自從首例「牛感」在六月於克爾克州被爆出，這波殺手級的感冒已經迅速向北邊，移動得比我們想像的還要快。在七月之前，幾乎國內的每一個地方都已經被「牛感」所攻擊。在短短兩個月之內，乳牛死亡的數量已攀升到 5,000 頭。雖然牛感是在南部開始的，但是國內的東部卻是受災最嚴重的地區。到本週為止，奧斯滕州 80% 的農場已回報有牛感案例。

因為牛感的關係，奧斯滕州的牛奶銷售額已<u>下降</u>。在牛感之前，奧斯滕州的每星期的牛奶銷售額為兩百五十萬美元；現在是低於五十萬美元。

奧丁州是在北部唯一沒有牛感案例的地方。在我們知道如何對付牛感之前，我們只能希望奧丁州將夠幸運，不用經歷這波殺手級流感的威力。

（伊蓮·貝克，城市郵報）

【註釋】

since〔sɪns〕*prep.* 自…以來；從…至今　　case〔kes〕*n.* 案例
cow〔kaʊ〕*n.* 母牛；乳牛　　cold〔kold〕*n.* 感冒

report〔rɪ'port〕*v. n.* 報告　　Kirk〔kɜk〕*n.* 克爾克
state〔stet〕*n.* 州　　June〔dʒun〕*n.* 六月
killer〔'kɪlɚ〕*n.* 殺人者；兇手　　***move up*** 向…挪動
north〔nɔrθ〕*adv.* 向北方；在北方　　July〔dʒu'laɪ〕*n.* 七月
attack〔ə'tæk〕*v.* 攻擊　　rise〔raɪz〕*v.* 上升；增加
the south　（一國、一地區之）南部
the east　（一國、一地區之）東部　　worst〔wɜst〕*adv.* 最嚴重地
hit〔hɪt〕*v.* 襲擊　　area〔'ɛrɪə〕*n.* 地區；區域
sale〔sel〕*n.* 銷售額　　slump〔slʌmp〕*v.*（物價等）下跌
because of 因為　　million〔'mɪljən〕*n.* 百萬
the north　（一國、一地區之）北部　　***deal with*** 應付；處理
lucky〔'lʌkɪ〕*adj.* 幸運的　　enough〔ə'nʌf〕*adv.* 足夠地
experience〔ɪk'spɪrɪəns〕*v.* 經歷　　power〔'paʊɚ〕*n.* 力量

32.（ **C** ）我們從該新聞報導中可得知什麼？

　　(A) 如何應付牛感。

　　(B) 人類是否有可能會得到牛感。

　　(C) 牛感襲擊該國的速度有多快。

　　(D) 如何發現乳牛是否感染牛感。

　　* news〔njuz〕*n.* 新聞；消息　　whether〔'hwɛðɚ〕*conj.* 是否
　　 catch〔kætʃ〕*v.* 感染　　***find out*** 找出；發現

33.（ **A** ）哪一張地圖將最有可能與上述新聞報導一起出現？

(A)　　　　　(B)　　　　　(C)　　　　　(D)

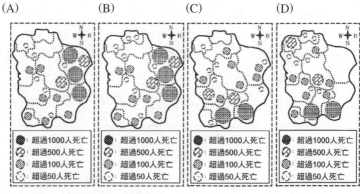

　　* appear〔ə'pɪr〕*v.* 出現

34.（ **A** ）如果商店的銷售額一直<u>下滑</u>，銷售圖表將會看起來如何？

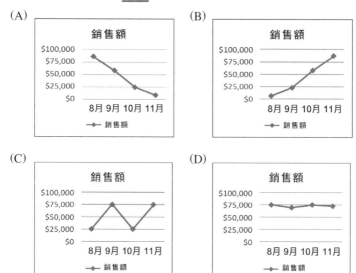

(A) 銷售額

(B) 銷售額

(C) 銷售額

(D) 銷售額

* **keep + V-ing** 持續…　　chart〔tʃɑrt〕n. 圖表；曲線圖

（35～38）

　　時間是晚上十一點，莫莉從她的麵包店走出來。她回頭看了她的那家店最後一次。她想要記住在那一刻它<u>看起來是什麼樣子</u>。
　　　　　　　　　　　　　　　　　　35
幾個小時後，就會有人來將店裡所有的東西都清除掉。有個年輕人把它買下來了。他<u>即將要把它變</u>成花店。
　　　　　　　　　　　　36
　　在成為麵包店之前，這個地方<u>以前是</u>間小型咖啡廳。莫莉在那
　　　　　　　　　　　　　　　37
裡擔任女服務生。但是接受點餐絕不是莫莉的夢想；烘培才是。當她知道她的老闆打算賣那家店，她就向朋友借錢把它買下來。
　　她的麵包店已經開了三十年了。這三十年真的很棒。不過，今

晚全都要結束了。莫莉<u>原本想要</u>把這間麵包店變成家族企業，但
　　　　　　　　 38
是她的女兒從未對烘培感興趣。莫莉不想要把她的事業交到陌生人
手中，所以經過認真思考後，她決定要結束營業。

　　「再見了，我親愛的老朋友，」莫莉看著這家店，低聲說道。

【註釋】

p.m. 下午　【比較】*a.m.* 上午　　*walk out of* 從…走出來
bakery〔'bekərɪ〕*n.* 麵包店　　turn〔tɜn〕*v.* 回頭　　*look at* 看
time〔taɪm〕*n.* 次數　　*one last time* 最後一次
remember〔rɪ'mɛmbə〕*v.* 記住
moment〔'momənt〕*n.* 時刻；片刻　　*a few* 一些；幾個
later〔'letə〕*adv.* …之後　　*clean out* 清理；清除
flower shop 花店　　*coffee shop* 咖啡廳
as〔æz〕*prep.* 以…身分；作為　　waitress〔'wetrɪs〕*n.* 女服務生
order〔'ɔrdə〕*n.* 點餐　　*take orders* 接受點餐
never〔'nɛvə〕*adv.* 從未；絕不；絕非
dream〔drim〕*n.* 夢想　　baking〔'bekɪŋ〕*n.* 烘烤；烘培
boss〔bɔs〕*n.* 老闆　　*plan to V.* 打算…
sell〔sɛl〕*v.* 賣　　borrow〔'baro〕*v.* 借（入）
open〔'opən〕*adj.* 開著的；營業中的
wonderful〔'wʌndəfəl〕*adj.* 很棒的
however〔hau'ɛvə〕*adv.* 然而　　*come to an end* 結束
business〔'bɪznɪs〕*n.* 生意；事業；企業
family business 家族企業　　*be interested in* 對…有興趣
stranger〔'strendʒə〕*n.* 陌生人　　serious〔'sɪrɪəs〕*adj.* 認真的
thinking〔'θɪŋkɪŋ〕*n.* 思考　　decide〔dɪ'saɪd〕*v.* 決定
close〔kloz〕*v.* 關閉；使停止營業　　dear〔dɪr〕*adj.* 親愛的
whisper〔'hwɪspə〕*v.* 低語

---

35. (**B**) 依句意，「要記住它在那一刻看起來的樣子」，動詞應用過去
　　　式，故選 (B) *looked like*「看起來像」。

36.（**C**）有個年輕人把它買下來，「即將要把」它「改」成花店，選
　　　　（C）*was going to change*。　　*be going to V.* 將要…

37.（**A**）這裡「以前是」一間小型的咖啡廳，選 (A) *used to be*。
　　　　used to V. 以前…
　　　　【比較】*be used to + V-ing* 習慣於…

38.（**A**）依句意，莫莉「原本想要」把這間麵包店變成家族企業，表
　　　　「過去未實現的希望或計畫」，要用「過去完成式」，選 (A)
　　　　had wanted。(詳見「文法寶典」p.338)

（39～41）

> 　　「家庭」這個字對你來說有何意義呢？一項 2006 年的美國研究
> 顯示，今日的人們<u>對於家庭的構成要素有幾種不同的想法</u>。超過百分
> 　　　　　　　　　　　　　　　　39
> 之 99 的受訪者同意，有丈夫、太太和小孩，就是一個家庭。同時，百
> 分之 94 的人認為父母親其中一人和小孩也是家庭，百分之 91 的人說，
> 只有夫妻沒有小孩也是家庭，還有百分之 81 的人認為，一男一女帶著
> 小孩，但是沒有結婚，也是家庭。
> 　　這項研究也發現，<u>人們是否有小孩</u>，在現代有關家庭的想法中
> 　　　　　　　　　　　　40
> 相當重要。雖然百分之 81 的人認為，一男一女沒有結婚帶著小孩，
> 算是家庭，但如果這對伴侶沒有小孩，百分比就降到百分之 40。這
> 個想法也適用於同性伴侶。大約有百分之 60 的人認為，兩男或兩女
> 帶著小孩，算是家庭，但如果這對伴侶沒有小孩，就只有百分之 32
> 的人這麼認為了。
> 　　在這項研究中，認為兩男或兩女住在一起算是家庭的人，通常
> 也贊成同性伴侶結婚。<u>這不令人驚訝</u>。然而，並非每個人都能展開
> 　　　　　　　　　　　41
> 雙臂接受同性伴侶：研究提到，百分之 30 的人將寵物視為家庭成員
> 沒問題，但他們不認為同性伴侶是家庭。

【註釋】

mean〔 min 〕 *v.* 意謂著　　study〔'stʌdɪ 〕 *n.* 研究
interview〔'ɪntə‚vju 〕 *v.* 面試；訪談
agree〔 ə'gri 〕 *v.* 同意　　***at the same time*** 同時
see A as B 認為 A 是 B　　married〔'mærɪd 〕 *adj.* 結婚的
modern〔'mɑdən 〕 *adj.* 現代的
thinking〔'θɪŋkɪŋ 〕 *n.* 思考；想法
percentage〔 pə'sɛntɪdʒ 〕 *n.* 百分比
drop〔 drɑp 〕 *v.* 下降　　couple〔'kʌpl 〕 *n.* 伴侶
sex〔 sɛks 〕 *n.* 性別　　same-sex *adj.* 同性的
find〔 faɪnd 〕 *v.* 覺得　　pet〔 pɛt 〕 *n.* 寵物
open one's arms 張開雙臂

39. (**D**) (A) 對於何時生小孩想法不同
　　　　　(B) 不像他們的父母一樣認為家庭很重要
　　　　　(C) 在開始生小孩時想要有許多不同的事物
　　　　　(D) 對於家庭的構成要素有幾種不同的想法
　　　　　* ***start a family*** 開始生兒育女　　make〔 mek 〕 *v.* 構成

40. (**B**) (A) 人們是否有結婚
　　　　　(B) 人們是否有小孩
　　　　　(C) 人們是否住在一起
　　　　　(D) 人們是否彼此相愛
　　　　　* ***whether…or ont*** 是否　　***each other*** 彼此

41. (**A**) (A) 這不令人驚訝
　　　　　(B) 這並非每個地方都可能
　　　　　(C) 這對每個人都不是好消息
　　　　　(D) 這個樣子不可能持續很久的時間

聽力測驗（第 1-21 題，共 21 題）

第一部分：辨識句意（第 1-3 題，共 3 題）

1. (**A**) (A)　　　　　　(B)　　　　　　(C)

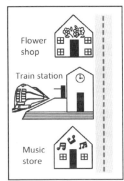
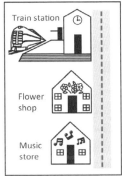

The train station is between a flower shop and a music store. 火車站在花店和唱片行中間。

* station〔ˋsteʃən〕*n.* 車站　　*train station* 火車站
　shop〔ʃɑp〕*n.* 商店　　*flower shop* 花店
　music store 唱片行

2. (**C**) (A)　　　　　　(B)　　　　　　(C)

In the race, two of the five runners got to the finish line at the same time.
在這比賽，五位賽跑者有兩位同時到達終點線。

* race〔res〕*n.* 比賽；賽跑　　runner〔ˋrʌnɚ〕*n.* 賽跑者
　get to 到達　　*finish line* 終點線
　at the same time 同時

3. (**C**) (A)　　　　　　(B)　　　　　　(C)

Sam almost finished his salad and steak, but didn't touch the bread at all.

山姆幾乎吃完了沙拉和牛排，但是他完全沒有碰麵包。

* almost〔'ɔl,most〕*adv.* 幾乎　　finish〔'fɪnɪʃ〕*v.* 吃完
salad〔'sæləd〕*n.* 沙拉　　steak〔stek〕*n.* 牛排
touch〔tʌtʃ〕*v.* 碰；接觸；吃（喝）　　bread〔brɛd〕*n.* 麵包
not~at all 一點也不~；完全沒有~

第二部分：基本問答（第 4-10 題，共 7 題）

4. (**B**) May I have your number so I can call you later?
可以給我你的電話，這樣我以後可以打電話給你嗎？

(A) It's 12:30. 現在是十二點三十分。

(B) It's 2345-6789. 號碼是 2345-6789。

(C) It's May 26, 1998. 今天是 1998 年，5 月 26 日。

* number〔'nʌmbɚ〕*n.* 電話號碼　　call〔kɔl〕*v.* 打電話給
later〔'letɚ〕*adv.* 以後

5. (**C**) Did you watch TV last night? 你昨天晚上有看電視嗎？

(A) So did I. 我也有。

(B) Thanks for telling me. 謝謝你告訴我。

(C) No. Any big news? 沒有。有任何重要的新聞嗎？

* ***watch TV*** 看電視　　***thanks for***~ 謝謝~
big〔bɪg〕*adj.* 重要的　　news〔njuz〕*n.* 新聞

6. (**C**) Could you turn off the radio?　I'm trying to study.

你可以把收音機關掉嗎？我正準備讀書。

(A) Get ready.　準備好。

(B) Good job.　做得好。

(C) No problem.　<u>沒問題。</u>

* ***turn off*** 關掉（電器）　　radio〔ˋredɪͺo〕*n.* 收音機
try〔traɪ〕*v.* 嘗試　　study〔ˋstʌdɪ〕*v.* 讀書
get ready 準備好　　***Good job.*** 做得好。
No problem. 好的；沒問題。

7. (**B**) This restaurant is lovely and the food we just had was excellent.　We should come again.

這間餐廳很美麗，而且我們剛吃的食物很棒。我們應該要再來。

(A) I know!　You cooked well.　我知道！你很會煮飯。

(B) Yes, I knew you'd like it.　<u>是的，我知道你會喜歡。</u>

(C) When did you order the food?　你什麼時候點菜的？

* restaurant〔ˋrɛstərənt〕*n.* 餐廳
lovely〔ˋlʌvlɪ〕*adj.* 美麗的；可愛的；極好的
just〔dʒʌst〕*adv.* 剛剛　　have〔hæv〕*v.* 吃；喝
excellent〔ˋɛksḷənt〕*n.* 很棒的
cook〔kʊk〕*v.* 煮飯；烹飪　　order〔ˋɔrdɚ〕*v.* 點（菜）

8. (**A**) Excuse me.　I believe this is your wallet.

對不起。我想這是你的皮夾。

(A) Oh, thank you.　<u>喔，謝謝你。</u>

(B) Oh, excuse me.　喔，對不起。

(C) Oh, you're lucky.　喔，你真幸運。

* ***excuse me*** 對不起【用於引起注意】
believe〔bɪˋliv〕*v.* 相信；認為　　wallet〔ˋwalɪt〕*n.* 皮夾
oh〔o〕*interj.*（表示驚訝、喜悅等）喔；啊；哎呀
lucky〔ˋlʌkɪ〕*adj.* 幸運的

9. (**B**) Where are you going to meet up with Candy?

你要去哪裡和坎迪碰面？

(A) After school. 放學後。

(B) At the park. 在公園。

(C) In the refrigerator. 在冰箱裡面。

* ***be going to V.*** 即將～；正要～

meet up with 和～碰頭；和～相聚　　***after school*** 放學後

park〔park〕*n.* 公園　　refrigerator〔rɪˈfrɪdʒə͵retə〕*n.* 冰箱

10. (**A**) The Moon Festival is only two weeks away!

離中秋節只要再兩週！

(A) I can't wait. 我等不及了。

(B) It didn't take long. 那不用很久。

(C) That's too slow. 那太慢了。

* ***the Moon Festival*** 中秋節（ = *the Mid Autumn Festival*）

away〔əˈwe〕*adv.* (時間) 離開；相隔

wait〔wet〕*v.* 等待　　take〔tek〕*v.* 花 (時間)

long〔lɔŋ〕*n.* 長時間　　slow〔slo〕*adj.* 慢的

第三部分：言談理解（第 11-21 題，共 11 題）

11. (**B**) W：I like music and movies. And you?

女：我喜歡音樂和電影。你呢？

M：I like swimming and playing basketball.

男：我喜歡游泳和打籃球。

Question：What does the man like? 男士喜歡什麼？

(A) Science. 科學。

(B) Sports. 運動。

(C) Reading. 閱讀。

* like〔laɪk〕*v.* 喜歡　　science〔ˈsaɪəns〕*n.* 科學

12. (**A**) W：I'm going to Ing-ying School.

　　　女：我要去應英學校。

　　　M：On Park Road?

　　　男：在公園路上的？

　　　W：That's right.

　　　女：對。

　　　M：Here we are.

　　　男：我們到了。

　　　W：Thank you. How much is that?

　　　女：謝謝你。多少錢。

　　　M：Seventy-five dollars.

　　　男：七十五元。

　　　Question：What is the man? 男士是做什麼的？

　　　(A) A taxi driver. 一位計程車司機。

　　　(B) A shopkeeper. 一位商店老闆。

　　　(C) A police officer. 一位警察。

　　　* taxi〔'tæksɪ〕*n.* 計程車　　driver〔'draɪvɚ〕*n.* 司機
　　　　shopkeeper〔'ʃɑp͵kipɚ〕*n.* 商店老闆

13. (**C**) W：What's that smell?

　　　女：那是什麼味道？

　　　M：Umm… Where is it coming from?

　　　男：嗯…它是從哪裡來的？

　　　W：Anything on your shoes?

　　　女：你的鞋子上有任何東西嗎？

　　　M：Nope. Maybe the trash can?

　　　男：沒有。也許是垃圾桶？

　　　W：Don't think so. I took out the garbage yesterday.

　　　女：不認為是。我昨天把垃圾拿出去了。

M：Oh, it's Tom's noodles! I think that bowl has been there for days.

男：噢，是湯姆的麵！我想那個碗已經在哪裡幾天了。

Question：Where does the smell come from?

味道是從哪裡來的？

(A) The man's shoes. 男士的鞋子。

(B) The trash can. 垃圾桶。

(C) Tom's noodles. 湯姆的麵。

* smell〔smɛl〕*n.* 味道　　***trash can*** 垃圾桶

garbage〔'gɑrbɪdʒ〕*n.* 垃圾

14. (**B**) M：Susan, nice to meet you.

男：蘇珊，很高興認識妳。

W：Nice to meet you, too. My brother always talks about you. He says you are his best friend.

女：我也很高興認識你。我的兄弟總是談到你。

他說你是他最好的朋友。

M：Yeah, Ted and I are good friends.

男：是的，泰德和我是好朋友。

Question：Who's Susan? 蘇珊是誰？

(A) Ted's mother. 泰德的母親。

(B) Ted's sister. 泰德的姊妹。

(C) Ted's friend. 泰德的朋友。

* meet〔mit〕*v.* 會見；碰面　　***talk about*** 談到

15. (**A**) M：Good evening, everyone. Welcome to John's Favorite Time. Joining me today is Anna Richards.

男：大家晚安。歡迎來到約翰的最愛時刻。今天加入我的是安娜・理查斯。

W : Hello, John. It's a pleasure to be here. What I'm going to show you today is Italian chicken.

女：哈囉，約翰。到這裡是我的榮幸。我今天要向你展示的是義大利雞。

M : Hmm, sounds good!

男：嗯，聽起來不錯！

W : And it tastes good, too. Now, you'll need four chicken legs. You'll also need two eggs, butter, tomatoes, cheese, and…

女：它嚐起來也很好吃。現在，你需要四支雞腿。你還需要兩顆蛋、奶油、蕃茄、起司，和…。

Question : What is the woman going to do?

女士正要做什麼？

(A) Cooking food. 烹飪食物。

(B) Making a shopping list. 製作購物清單。

(C) Buying dinner for the man. 替男士買晚餐。

* favorite〔'fevərɪt〕*adj.* 最喜愛的

　Italian〔ɪ'tæljən〕*adj.* 義大利的

　sound〔saʊnd〕*v.* 聽起來　　taste〔test〕*v.* 嚐起來

16. (**B**) Welcome to Bernard House. The program will begin in fifteen minutes. If you want to use the restroom, turn left when you walk out of the room. Please don't drink or eat inside. Be sure to turn off your cell phone, and don't take photos during the show. We hope you have a wonderful time tonight.

歡迎來到柏納德戲院。節目會在十五分鐘內開始。如果你想要使用洗手間，走出房間後左轉。院內請勿飲食。務必關掉你的手機，並且不要在表演時拍照。我們希望今晚你會有個美好的時刻。

Question : What is Bernard House? 柏納德戲院是什麼？

(A) A library. 一間圖書館。

(B) A theater. 一間戲院。

(C) A restaurant. 一間餐廳。

* house〔haʊs〕*n.* 戲院
program〔'progræm〕*n.* 節目
begin〔bɪ'gɪn〕*v.* 開始　　sure〔ʃʊr〕*adj.* 必定的
turn off 關掉　　show〔ʃo〕*n.* 表演

17. (**A**) W : Hi, I'm Ellie, the head of Dreamer. You must be Paul. Tell me something about your work experience.

女：嗨，我是艾莉，夢想家的總經理。你一定就是保羅。
告訴我一些關於你的工作經驗。

M : Sure. I worked as a waiter for three years.

男：好的。我擔任過服務生三年。

W : Don't you think it's tiring to be a waiter?

女：你不覺得當服務生很累嗎？

M : Not at all. I love food and I like to see people enjoying their meals.

男：一點也不。我喜歡食物，而且我喜歡看人們享用他們的餐點。

W : Good. Can you tell me more about...

女：很好。你可以告訴我更多關於…

Question : What are the man and woman doing?

男士和女士在做什麼？

(A) Having a job interview. 進行工作面試。

(B) Ordering their food. 點餐。

(C) Talking about some news. 談論一些新聞。

* Ellie〔'ɛlɪ〕*n.*（女子名）艾莉　　head〔hɛd〕*n.* 總經理
dreamer〔'drimɚ〕*n.* 做夢的人；夢想家
Paul〔pɔl〕*n.* 保羅　　sure〔ʃʊr〕*adv.* 當然；沒問題

experience〔ɪkˈspɪrɪəns〕*n.* 經驗　　***work as*** 擔任
waiter〔ˈwetɚ〕*n.* 服務生　　tiring〔ˈtaɪrɪŋ〕*adj.* 累人的
food〔fud〕*n.* 食物　　enjoy〔ɪnˈdʒɔɪ〕*v.* 享受
meal〔mil〕*n.* 餐點　　job〔dʒɑb〕*n.* 工作
interview〔ˈɪntɚˌvju〕*n.* 面試　　order〔ˈɔrdɚ〕*v.* 點（菜）
talk about 談論　　news〔njuz〕*n.* 新聞

18.（**A**）(Phone rings)

（電話響）

M：Hello!

男：哈囉！

W：Hello, Sam. Where are you guys? I've been waiting for twenty minutes.

女：哈囉，山姆。你們在哪？我已經等了二十分鐘了。

M：I'm on the bus. Are you already at the museum?

男：我在公車上。你已經在博物館了嗎？

W：The museum? I'm at the school gate! I thought we were meeting here at nine.

女：博物館？我在學校大門口！我以為我們九點在這裡會面。

M：No! We are meeting at the museum at ten.

男：不！我們要十點在博物館會面。

W：What?! Who decided that?

女：什麼？！是誰決定那樣的？

M：Didn't Tom call you last night?

男：湯姆昨天晚上沒有打電話給妳嗎？

W：No, he did not.

女：不，他沒有。

Question：Why is the girl at the school gate?

　　　　　為什麼女孩在校門口？

(A) She did not know the plan had been changed.

　　她不知道計畫已經變了。

(B) She is waiting for the bus to the museum.

　　她正在等去博物館的公車。

(C) She made a mistake about where to meet.

　　她搞錯要會面的地方。

* phone〔fon〕*n.* 電話　　ring〔rɪŋ〕*v.* (鈴) 響
wait〔wet〕*v.* 等待<*for*>　　minute〔ˈmɪnɪt〕*n.* 分鐘
already〔ɔlˈrɛdɪ〕*adv.* 已經
museum〔mjuˈziəm〕*n.* 博物館　　gate〔get〕*n.* 大門
meet〔mit〕*v.* 見面；會面　　decide〔dɪˈsaɪd〕*v.* 決定
call〔kɔl〕*v.* 打電話給　　plan〔plæn〕*n.* 計畫
change〔tʃendʒ〕*v.* 改變　　mistake〔məˈstek〕*n.* 錯誤
make a mistake 犯錯

19. (**C**)　M：Sophie, is everything going well at school? It's been
　　　　　　two weeks, right?

　　男：蘇菲，上課一切都好嗎？兩個星期了，對吧？

　　W：Yeah. I've met three classmates who love drawing
　　　　pictures, just like me!

　　女：是啊。我認識了三位像我一樣喜歡畫圖的同學！

　　M：How about classes?

　　男：課程如何？

　　W：Well, most of them are interesting, but I have much
　　　　more homework here than at my last school.

　　女：嗯，大部分的課都很有趣，但是比我上一間學校多了許多
　　　　家庭作業。

　　Question：What can we know about Sophie?

　　　　　　　關於蘇菲，我們可以知道什麼？

(A) She feels lonely at school. 她在學校感到寂寞。

(B) She's not interested in drawing pictures.

　　她對畫圖不感興趣。

(C) She's just started going to a new school.

　　<u>她正剛開始去新學校上學。</u>

* ***at school*** 在上課　　draw〔drɔ〕*v.* 畫；繪製

　interesting〔'ɪntərɪstɪŋ〕*adj.* 有趣的

　lonely〔'lonlɪ〕*adj.* 寂寞的

　be interested in　對…感興趣

20. (**A**)　W：That was a great movie! I loved it!

　　　　女：那真是一部好電影！我愛它！

　　　　M：Seriously? It was as exciting as watching paint dry.

　　　　男：真的嗎？看這部電影就像是看油漆乾掉一樣令人興奮。

　　　　W：Really? Why?

　　　　女：真的嗎？為什麼？

　　　　M：I knew who the bad guy was from the start. Why did
　　　　　　we spend two hours waiting for them to find out?

　　　　男：我從一開始就知道誰是壞人。為什麼我們要花兩個小時等
　　　　　　他們去找出來？

　　　　Question：What does the woman think of the movie?

　　　　　　　　　女士認為這部電影怎麼樣？

　　　　(A) It was boring. <u>它很無聊。</u>

　　　　(B) It was exciting. 它很刺激。

　　　　(C) It was serious. 它很嚴肅。

　　　　* exciting〔ɪk'saɪtɪŋ〕*adj.* 令人興奮的

　　　　　paint〔pent〕*n.* 油漆　　guy〔gaɪ〕*n.* 傢伙；人

　　　　　start〔stɑrt〕*n.* 最初；開端　　***wait for*** 等候

　　　　　find out 找出；發現　　***think of*** 認為

21. (**B**)　(Applause) Wow! I can't believe I'm standing here. I'm
so happy! (Coughs and clears throat) Well, first, I'd like
to thank my parents. They paid for my acting classes for
so many years. Now I can tell them they didn't spend
their money for nothing. (Crowd laughs) My thanks also
go to the excellent team I've worked with. Special thanks
go to Andy, who wrote a great part for me. Also, I must
thank my husband, Eddie. He's done all the housework
and taken care of our baby. Without him I couldn't have
done so well on the big screen. Thank you. Thank you
all for believing in me. (Applause)

（鼓掌）哇！我不敢相信我站在這裡。我太高興了！（咳嗽和清
喉嚨）嗯，首先，我想感謝我的父母。他們付了我多年的演員課
程。現在我可以告訴他們，他們的錢沒有白花。（衆人笑）我也
感謝和我一起工作過的優秀團隊。特別感謝安迪，把我的角色寫
得很好。此外，我一定要感謝我的丈夫，艾迪。他做所有的家務，
並且照顧我們的寶貝。沒有他，我不可能在大銀幕上表現得這麼
好。謝謝。謝謝所有相信我的人。（鼓掌）

Question：What did the speaker win the prize for?
　　　　　說話者因為什麼而得獎？

(A) For her book. 她的書。

(B) For her movie. 她的電影。

(C) For her news report. 她的新聞報導。

* applause〔ə'plɔz〕*n.* 鼓掌；喝采
　cough〔kɔf〕*n.* 咳嗽聲　　throat〔θrot〕*n.* 喉嚨
　crowd〔kraʊd〕*n.* 群衆　　laugh〔læf〕*v.* 笑
　excellent〔'ɛksḷənt〕*adj.* 特優的

【劉毅英文製作】

105 年國中教育會考英語科修正意見

題　　號	修　　正　　意　　見
第 16–17 題 第 6 行	…at *Town Office*. → at **the Town Office**. (在鎮公所) * 原則上，專有名詞不加冠詞，但機關、學校、醫院、商店或其他公共建築物的名稱，要加 the，如：the White House（白宮）、the Ministery of Foreign Affairs（外交部）等。【詳見「文法寶典」p.62】
第 18–20 題 第二段 第 5 行	All year *around*…. → All year **round**…. * **all** (*the*) **year round**（一年到頭；終年），是 **round** 不是 *around*。
第 21–22 題 第 1 行	Here is the schedule *with the* notice *of* the summer school…. → Here is the schedule **and a** notice **from** the summer school…. * schedule（課表）和 notice（公告）是不同的東西。
第 22 題 第 2 行	Who can possibly *remember all of them in a night*? → Who can possibly **remember all of them**? 把句尾的 in a night 去掉。 或→ Who can possibly **memorize all of them in a night**? * 在英文中 remember 和 memorize 都作「記得」解，但是「在一夜之間背熟」，就要用 memorize。
第 23 題 (D)	He is afraid of being by himself when he feels *ghosts around*. → He is afraid of being by himself when he feels **ghosts are around**. * 在此 feels 相當於 thinks（認為），後面應加句子。feel 後面接名詞是成語，如：feel sympathy for（同情）。
第 25–27 題 第 10 張圖	*get* crazy first → **go** crazy first already *got crazy* → already **crazy** *「發瘋」是 go crazy，go 相當於 become。

第 31 題 (B)	"You never know what a girl like Olivia *would* want." → "You never know what a girl like Olivia **will** want." ＊依句意，應用未來式，不是過去的未來。
第 31–34 題 倒數第 2 行	*Before* we know how to deal with Cow Cold, we can only.... → **Until** we know how to deal with Cow Cold, we can only.... ＊Before 應改成 Until，Before 表「在…之前」，暗示治療方法一 　定能在某個時候找到，所以改成 Until 表「直到…的時候」，較 　符合句意。
第 35–38 題 第 1 行	It was 11p.m. *and* Molly walked out of her bakery. → It was 11p.m. ***when Molly walked out of her bakery.*** ＊依句意，「那時候」應用關係副詞 when 引導形容詞子句，修飾 　11p.m.。
倒數第 3 行	But her daughter *was never* interested in baking. → But her daughter **was not** interested in baking. 或→ But her daughter **had never been** interested in baking. ＊原則上，never 要和完成式連用。
第 36 題	He ___36___ it into a flower shop. (A) had *changed*　　　　　(B) *changed* (C) was going to *change*　(D) has *changed* → (A) had **turned**　　　　(B) **turned** 　　(C) was going to **turn**　(D) has **turned** ＊change A into B「把 A 變成 B」，是指本質與型態完全改變， 　和原來大不相同，例如：**chang**e the desert **into** farmland 　（把沙漠變成農地）。 　而 **turn** A **into** B「把 A 變成 B」，是將 A 發展成 B，例如：We 　**turned** one kind of business **into** another kind of business. 　（我們把一種事業變成另一種事業。）在此將 bakery（麵包店） 　變成 flowershop（花店），還是商店，所以應該用 **turn**...**into**。 　【例外】The prince was ｛ changed into ／ turned into ｝ a frog. 　　　　　（王子變成了青蛙。）

105 年度國中教育會考
英文科公佈答案

閱讀測驗

題　號	答　案
1	B
2	A
3	B
4	B
5	D
6	B
7	D
8	B
9	A
10	C
11	B
12	A
13	D
14	A
15	D
16	C
17	A
18	D
19	B
20	B
21	C

題　號	答　案
22	C
23	D
24	B
25	D
26	B
27	C
28	C
29	D
30	D
31	C
32	C
33	A
34	A
35	B
36	C
37	A
38	A
39	D
40	B
41	A

聽力測驗

題　號	答　案
1	A
2	C
3	C
4	B
5	C
6	C
7	B
8	A
9	B
10	A
11	B
12	A
13	C
14	B
15	A
16	B
17	A
18	A
19	C
20	A
21	B

心得筆記欄

104 年國中教育會考英語科試題

閱讀測驗（第 1-40 題，共 40 題）

第一部分：單題（第 1-12 題，共 12 題）

1. Look at the picture. The girl drew two
   _____ on the wall.
   (A) circles   (B) lines
   (C) points   (D) squares

2. This dress is pretty, _____ it does not look good on me.
   (A) so   (B) but
   (C) or   (D) if

3. Getting up early on a cold morning is not easy, _____?
   (A) are you   (B) do you
   (C) does it   (D) is it

4. Tonight I'll stay at the office until I _____ the work.
   (A) finish   (B) am finishing
   (C) finished   (D) will finish

5. Charles _____ a day in the department store looking for a hat for his wife.
   (A) cost   (B) spent
   (C) saw   (D) made

6. Tom _____ ten pounds over the past two months. He looks much thinner now.

   (A) loses   (B) has lost

   (C) will lose   (D) was losing

7. I don't like any one of these three watches. Can you show me _____ one?

   (A) the others   (B) other

   (C) either   (D) another

8. The waiters are asked to be _____; they should always smile and remember to say "Welcome" and "Please."

   (A) honest   (B) polite

   (C) special   (D) strong

9. On Children's Day, Ms. Lee, a famous storybook writer, _____ to Molly's Bookstore to talk about her new book. My two little kids just can't wait to see her.

   (A) came   (B) was coming

   (C) has come   (D) is going to come

10. No one thought James would appear at Katie's party. So when he _____, everyone was surprised and could not believe their eyes.

   (A) would   (B) was

   (C) had   (D) did

11. B&J Café _____ known as the tallest building in town.
    However, O&G Restaurant became the tallest building in
    2010.
    (A) has been   (B) had been
    (C) is   (D) would be

12. Actor David Piper became tired of talking about the movie
    _____ after he was interviewed about it many times.
    (A) he is famous   (B) that he is famous
    (C) that is famous for   (D) he is famous for

第二部分：題組（第 13-40 題，共 28 題）

（13-15）

From: Lisa Clyne (lisaclyne@mail.com)
To: Mary Faber (maryfaber@mail.com)
Date: Thursday, April 2, 2015
Subject: Welcome

Dear Mary,

Uncle Billy and I are excited about your visit.

The weather has ___13___ these days. Like today, it was

sunny in the morning, but rained heavily at noon. So we've

___14___: If the weather is nice, I'm going to take you to

Smith Farm. They're having a special horse show this week. I'm sure you'll like it. And __15__. We can go shopping at Mimi's Department Store; there we can walk around without getting wet. Rain or shine, we hope you will have a good time here.

See you tomorrow at the train station at 9:00 a.m.

Love,
Aunt Lisa

13. (A) got better
　　(B) been warm
　　(C) changed a lot
　　(D) become wet and cold

14. (A) made two plans for you
　　(B) worried about your trip to here
　　(C) decided to take you to a nice place
　　(D) prepared everything you've asked for

15. (A) we'll agree with each other
　　(B) don't worry if it rains
　　(C) we all love animals very much
　　(D) don't forget to check the weather

（16-18）

> **NEWS HUNT**
>
>
>
> --
>
> Kieran Hardy 11/07/2013
>
> For years, we thought our Earth was the only blue dot up there. Now another has been found. Its name is HD189773b. HD189773b is an exoplanet, a planet outside our Solar System, and is one of the nearest exoplanets to Earth. Even so, ___16___. Here's why: It is 63 light years away. That means it is 370,440,000,000,000 miles from us. Even if we fly at 3,500 miles an hour, it will take more than 12 million years to get there.
>
> ___17___: It is much bigger, it is made of gas and it is burning hot. In heat as great as 1,000℃, life is not possible. What is worse, it rains glass. If 1,000℃ docs not kill you, glass rain will.
>
> Even so, finding this blue giant ___18___. It is the first time that we have been able to see the color of an exoplanet. The color of a planet gives us ideas about what is happening on it. While we have a long way to go before we find a new planet to live on, finding a blue dot is a good start.
>
> 📖 exoplanet 系外行星　　Solar System 太陽系

16. (A) we cannot really call it a neighbor

    (B) we do not know anything about it yet

    (C) we might not be able to stay there for long

    (D) we are not sure how long it takes to get there

17. (A) What's more, it is not water that makes HD189773b look blue

    (B) With its blue color, HD189773b could be a second Earth for us

    (C) Except for its blue color, HD189773b is nothing like our home planet

    (D) Because of its blue color, people guess there might be life on HD189773b

18. (A) gives us hope

    (B) took hard work

    (C) has changed our life

    (D) helps us know more about Earth

(19-20)

Last Saturday, Ginny and her friends had lunch at Howell's Bowl. Here is their order, and the poster of the restaurant.

Howell's Bowl		
Table _2_　_3_ person(s)	Order taken by <u>Fred</u>	12:30 12/23
1	pumpkin pie	220 x 2
2	cheese cake	120 x 1
3	milk shake (chocolate) (large)	200 x 2
4	milk shake (banana)	110 x 1
5	chicken sandwich	100 x 1
6	chicken sandwich (with cheese)	120 x 1
7	cola (no ice)	65 x 1
8	orange juice (no ice)	90 x 1
9	grape juice	95 x 1
10		
	Total Price: $1,540	
Thank You & Hope to See You Soon!! Tel: XXX-XXXX		

Howell's Bowl

Open Hours:

11:30 am - 11:30 pm

Tues. to Sun.

Joy Time: 20% off

2:00 - 4:00 pm

9:30 - 11:30 pm

📖 poster 海報

19. On the order list, Ginny ordered a sandwich with cheese, a fruit milk shake, and a fruit drink without ice. How much did she have to pay for her food?
(A) $300.　　　　　　　　(B) $320.
(C) $385.　　　　　　　　(D) $410.

20. Ginny wants to go to Howell's Bowl again during Joy Time. When will she possibly go there?
(A) 11:00 a.m. on Wednesday.　(B) 2:30 p.m. on Monday.
(C) 8:00 p.m. on Friday.　　　(D) 10:00 p.m. on Thursday.

（21-23）

Below is how four students answered their teacher's question in class.

Lily　: I like shopping and talking to people. I think I can learn how to do business. Maybe selling clothes is a good business for me.

Ryan : My hobbies are playing computer games and making friends online. We often share our funny stories by e-mail. I guess I will learn more about computers and make super-smart computer programs.

Bill　: My parents have kept lots of pets since I was little. We've experienced many things together, good and bad, happy and sad. Those stories have always stayed in my mind. One day, I will share <u>them</u> with people by drawing and writing books.

Anna : Though my mom and two sisters are all doctors, I'm sure I will stay as far away from a hospital as I can. I hate being sick, and I'm afraid of seeing sick people looking weak and sad. I'll keep strong by playing my favorite sport, tennis, every day. One day I'll join the national team and be another Lu Yen-Hsun.

21. What question did the teacher most likely ask in class?

    (A) "What do you want to do in the future?"

    > 📖 likely　可能

    (B) "What's your plan for the coming vacation?"

    (C) "What do you like to talk about with your friends?"

    (D) "What's your favorite thing to do with your family?"

22. What do we know from the reading?

    (A) Lily is good at making clothes.

    (B) One of Bill's parents is an animal doctor.

    (C) Ryan enjoys meeting people on the Internet.

    (D) Anna was once very sick and stayed in the hospital for a long time.

23. What does <u>them</u> mean?

    (A) Pets.　　(B) Books.　　(C) Stories.　　(D) Parents.

（24-25）

Here is the preface of Nick Foster's new book *Married to Food*.

Preface

My mother was <u>lousy at</u> cooking. To her, cooking was more like an exciting experiment. You put some of this and some of that in a pot, and you wait and see what will happen. "No experiments, no experiences." is what she would say when her experiment did not turn out good, and I heard that a lot.

My father was a good cook, and he loved to cook, too. He often said that he got my mother to marry him with a table of delicious food, not with a beautiful ring. "A family needs only one good cook," he said.

Now I am a cook myself. And I have my own restaurant. I learned how to cook from my father, of course. From him, I learned the art of cooking. But I did learn one thing from my mother. It's her famous saying: "No experiments, no experiences."

iv

📖 preface 前言　　experiment 實驗

24. What does it mean when someone is <u>lousy at</u> something?
    (A) They are famous for it.
    (B) They cannot do it well.
    (C) They think it is important.
    (D) They are not interested in it.

25. What can we learn from the preface?
    (A) How Foster started his own restaurant.
    (B) When Foster's father married Foster's mother.
    (C) What Foster's mother taught him about cooking.
    (D) How Foster learned the art of cooking from his father.

（26-27）

Here are the rules for a game called "Trip to Dreamland."

1. Each player begins at **START**.

2. In each turn, first take one of the four cards 🌙 ❄ ☼ 🌢 to decide how many spaces to move: 🌙 for one space, ❄ for two spaces, ☼ for three spaces, and 🌢 for four spaces. Then follow the words next to the ☞, if there is a ☞ at the place you arrive at.

3. The first one who gets to Dreamland wins the game.

📖 turn 回合　　space 步、格

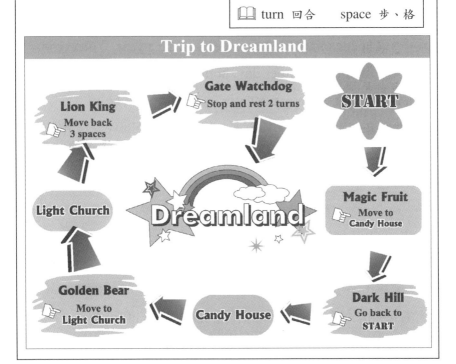

Trip to Dreamland

Lion King ☞ Move back 3 spaces

Gate Watchdog ☞ Stop and rest 2 turns

START

Light Church

Dreamland

Magic Fruit ☞ Move to Candy House

Golden Bear ☞ Move to Light Church

Candy House

Dark Hill ☞ Go back to START

26. Below are the cards which four kids have taken since they began the game. Who has won the game?
    (A) Anna: 🌙 → ☀ → 💧.　　(B) Kate: ❄ → ☀ → 💧.
    (C) Billy: 🌙 → ❄ → ☀.　　(D) Ivan: ❄ → 💧 → 🌙.

27. What can we learn about the game?
    (A) One can never begin his turn from Lion King.
    (B) The cards can be used to decide who goes first.
    (C) One can never get to Light Church at the first turn.
    (D) The cards can be used to decide where to start the game.

(28-31)

The idea may hit you once or twice a year. You come home on a hot summer day, hoping to have a cool bath, and find out there is no water. Then you see how important water is in your everyday life. However, in many parts of the world, water is not just about one's everyday need.

In countries like Tanzania, water is hard to get, and the job of collecting water falls on women's shoulders. Girls are often kept home from school to collect water while their brothers stay at school studying. Studies show Tanzanian girls who live 15 minutes from clean water spend 12% more time at school than those who live an hour away. More time spent collecting water means less time for learning. For these girls, "Knowledge is power" is not just words; it is a sad fact in real life. With less time spent at school, their chances of getting well-paid jobs are small, and they often have no voice in important matters, like who to marry. These girls are often married into poor families. They have little money or knowledge to take care of their children, who often end up dying young. For the baby girls who are lucky enough to live, their life may still center around "water," just like it did for their mothers.

28. What does The idea mean in the reading?
   (A) Water is important in one's everyday life.
   (B) Water is not just about one's everyday needs.
   (C) It is nice to have a cool bath on a hot summer day.
   (D) We should not take a bath when there is little water.

29. What is the reading mostly about?
   (A) Why it is important to save water.
   (B) How water may give a country power.
   (C) How water may play a part in one's future.
   (D) Why it is hard to get water in poor countries.

30. What do we know from the reading?

(A) Children in poor countries die from drinking dirty water every day.

(B) Girls who spend little time at school have a harder life when they grow up.

(C) Girls in countries like Tanzania are often paid less for the same job than the boys are.

(D) Children from poor families are often kept from school to take care of younger children.

31. Families in the countries of Benin, Ghana, Guinea and Madagascar deal with the job of water-collecting the same way Tanzanian families do. From the reading, which chart best shows the fact?　📖 chart 圖表

(A)
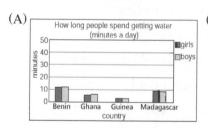

(B)
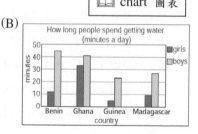

(C)
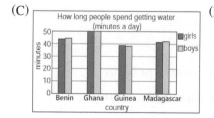

(D)
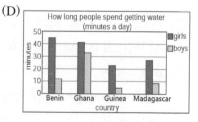

（32-34）

(At Liz's birthday party)

Amber : Don't tell me you didn't go to <u>Garden House</u>.

Keith　: Why would I go there?

Amber : For Liz's birthday cake! I left you a voice message this morning!

Keith　: But you said Matt would go to the bakery! And why did you come here without me? I was waiting outside your apartment for an hour!

Amber : No! I said I'd have lunch with Matt, and we'd come straight here from the restaurant. So I asked you to help get the cake after work.

Keith　: No, you did not! And why didn't you answer my calls?

Amber : My cellphone is dead! I said in the message that you could call Matt's number if you wanted to find me. Now please tell me you did bring the gift we got for Liz.

Keith　: What gift? I'm sure you didn't say anything about a gift in the message.

Amber : I told you that yesterday!

📖 message 留言

32. What is <u>Garden House</u>?

   (A) A bakery.

   (B) A gift shop.

   (C) A flower shop.

   (D) An apartment.

33. What can we learn about Keith?

   (A) He forgot to meet Amber and Matt for lunch.

   (B) He did not know how to get to Amber's apartment.

   (C) He called Amber without knowing her phone was not working.

   (D) He did not know Amber left him a voice message this morning.

34. Which sentence was most likely part of the message that Amber left Keith this morning?

> 📖 likely 可能

   (A) "Matt and I will go to the party after lunch."

   (B) "Don't forget to buy a birthday gift for Liz."

   (C) "You can go straight to the party from your office."

   (D) "I need to talk to you about the party this weekend."

（35-36）

　　Froggie was a frog who never remembered where he had been. His biggest dream was to find the best pond to swim freely without worrying about water snakes. One day, Froggie hopped to a kitchen and jumped into a pot full of hot water. Froggie felt the burning heat and hurried out of the water as fast as his legs could carry him. "I almost died there!" Froggie thought.

　　A few days later, Froggie went back to the same kitchen, totally forgetting he had been there. He again hopped into the same pot. This time, the water inside was cool. He looked around and thought, "There's no water snake trying to eat me and I can have this place all to myself!" At that moment, Froggie knew it was his dream pond. What he didn't know was that the water was warming up over a low heat.

　　After thirty minutes of swimming, Froggie felt the water was warmer but he thought of this as a nice surprise. "This sure is the best place for swimming. I get to have a hot bath, too." During his comfortable bath, the water kept getting warmer and warmer. Froggie was so comfortable that he fell asleep. And he never woke up.

35. What lesson can we learn from Froggie's story?

    (A) Life is too short; one should live it to the fullest.

    (B) Those who use their time well will win in the end.

    (C) People are blind to problems that slowly get worse over time.

    (D) It is difficult to give up old habits, but easy to pick up new ones.

36. What do we know about Froggie?

    (A) He learned to share what he liked with others.

    (B) He thought what he had hoped for became real.

    (C) He once almost lost a dear friend to a water snake.

    (D) He wanted to go back to the same pot for a hot bath.

(37-40)

The Metro Times

Oct. 1. 2020

These years churches are <u>in a calamitous state</u>. To start with, the number of church-goers is dropping sharply (see Figure 1). Many say they do not belong to any church, and those who do go less often than they used to. Going to church appears less and less on people's to-do list. Another worrying fact is that fewer and fewer young people go to church, which leads to an older church (see Figure 2).

And there is also the problem with money. Keeping a church door open is not cheap. Fewer people going to church means little money coming in. This makes it harder to keep a church open.

When the time comes for a church to close, there is little to do but to sell it. Churches that were lucky enough to find a buyer were put to other uses. Some were changed into restaurants or school gyms, and some even became nightclubs, for example. Churches that had little luck were knocked down in the end.

Just like a store that keeps losing business needs to think of ways to save itself, it is perhaps time for the church to try to win people's hearts back and play an important part in people's lives again. This is not something that one can simply pray to get an answer to.

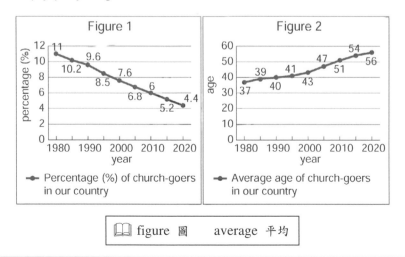

Figure 1	Figure 2
Percentage (%) of church-goers in our country	Average age of church-goers in our country

📖 figure 圖　　average 平均

37. What does it mean when someone <u>is in a calamitous state</u>?
    (A) They have serious trouble.
    (B) They try to change themselves.
    (C) They are looking for a second chance.
    (D) They lost interest in the outside world.

38. What can we learn about the church-goers from the report?
    (A) Between 1980 and 2005, few church-goers were younger than 50.
    (B) In 2010, only 6% of church-goers were younger than 50 years old.
    (C) In 2020, the percentage (%) of church-goers drops to lower than half that in 1980.
    (D) Between 1980 and 2020, the rising number of old church-goers has led to an old church.

39. What is talked about in the report?
    (A) Where the church's money goes.
    (B) How people decide to join a church.
    (C) What happens to churches that are closed.
    (D) Why people have stopped going to church.

40. Below are four findings from other reports. Which does NOT agree with the idea of the report?

(A) "Reports show over 90% of church-goers go to church because their fathers do. In the last 20 years, 49% of men under 30 have left the church. That means there's a 90% chance that their children won't go to church. This is hard for the church to take in."

(B) "Between 2003 and 2010, over 1,000 new churches were built in the country. This may sound like good news. During the same years, however, more than 2,000 were closed."

(C) "In the report, 33% of the people that were interviewed say they never go to church and another 33% say they used to. Only 15% go to church at least once a month."

(D) "Of the 15 countries in the report, the percentage (%) of church-goers in some countries, like Denmark, is lower than 10%; in others, like Poland, the percentage is higher than 70%."

聽力測驗（第 1-21 題，共 21 題）

第一部分：辨識句意（第 1-3 題，共 3 題）

作答說明： 第 1-3 題每題有三張圖片，請依據所聽到的內容，選出符合描述的圖片，每題播放兩次。

示例題：你會看到

(A) 　　　(B) 　　　(C)

然後你會聽到……（播音）。依據所播放的內容，正確答案應該選 A，請將答案卡該題「Ⓐ」的地方塗黑、塗滿，即：● Ⓑ Ⓒ

1. (A) 　　(B) 　　(C)

2. (A) (B) (C)

3. (A) (B) (C)

第二部分：基本問答（第 4-10 題，共 7 題）

作答說明： 第 4-10 題每題均有三個選項，請依據所聽到的內容，選出一個最適合的回應，每題播放兩次。

示例題：你會看到

(A) She is talking to the teacher.

(B) She is a student in my class.

(C) She is wearing a beautiful dress.

然後你會聽到……（播音）。依據所播放的內容，正確答案應該選 B，請將答案卡該題「Ⓑ」的地方塗黑、塗滿，即：Ⓐ ● Ⓒ

---

4. (A) Since when?
   (B) Almost there.
   (C) No problem.

5. (A) I got it from my grandparents.
   (B) L-I-N-D-Y.
   (C) My name is Lindy.

6. (A) Sorry. I need it right now.
   (B) Thanks. You're very nice.
   (C) I already have one.

7. (A) Give me five more minutes.
   (B) It's not early enough.
   (C) The taxi driver will be late.

8. (A) I can't believe you got the job!
   (B) What a small world!
   (C) You're really lucky!

9. (A) I'll be out in a minute.
   (B) Sorry. Let me help you.
   (C) You don't have much time.

10 (A) I'm happy to hear that.
   (B) That's a good idea.
   (C) That's too bad.

第三部分：言談理解（第 11-21 題，共 11 題）

作答說明： 第 11-21 題每題均有三個選項，請依據所聽到的內容，選出一個最適合的答案，每題播放兩次。

示例題：你會看到

(A) 9:50.　　(B) 10:00.　　(C) 10:10.

然後你會聽到……（播音）。依據所播放的內容，正確答案應該選 B，請將答案卡該題「Ⓑ」的地方塗黑、塗滿，即：Ⓐ ● Ⓒ

---

11. (A) Coffee.
    (B) Water.
    (C) Tea.

12. (A) Shoes.
    (B) A ball.
    (C) A dress.

13. (A) The skirt will be on sale next week.
    (B) The skirt is too expensive for her to buy.
    (C) The skirt is too long for her.

14. (A) Ask for her money back.
    (B) Choose a different book.
    (C) Wait for the new order.

15. (A) In a bank.
    (B) In a police station.
    (C) In a post office.

16. (A) A museum that collects old things.
    (B) A supermarket that sells cheaper things.
    (C) A shop that sells old things.

17. (A) She doesn't really like it.
    (B) She is excited about it.
    (C) She knows nothing about it.

18. (A) He got lost in the train station.
    (B) He got off at the wrong station.
    (C) He took the wrong train.

19. (A) She may be too lazy.
    (B) She may not like him.
    (C) She may have to stay home.

20. (A) 10:00.
    (B) 11:00.
    (C) 12:00.

21. (A) I Still Believe.
    (B) Listen to Your Heart.
    (C) Slow Dance.

104年國中教育會考英語科試題詳解

閱讀測驗（第1-40題，共40題）

第一部分：單題（第1-12題，共12題）

1.(**D**) 看圖片。女孩在牆上畫了兩個<u>正方形</u>。

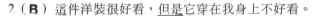

      (A) circle〔ˋsɝkḷ〕*n.* 圓
      (B) line〔laɪn〕*n.* 線
      (C) point〔pɔɪnt〕*n.* 點
      (D) *square*〔skwɛr〕*n.* 正方形
      * picture〔ˋpɪktʃɚ〕*n.* 圖片   draw〔drɔ〕*v.* 畫

2.(**B**) 這件洋裝很好看，<u>但是</u>它穿在我身上不好看。

      (A) so〔so〕*conj.* 所以   (B) *but*〔bʌt〕*conj.* 但是
      (C) or〔ɔr〕*conj.* 或者   (D) if〔ɪf〕*conj.* 如果
      * dress〔drɛs〕*n.* 洋裝   look〔lʊk〕*v.* 看起來

3.(**D**) 在寒冷的早晨早起是不容易的，<u>是嗎</u>？

      前後否定，附加問句須用肯定，且須用 be 動詞 is，又主詞為
      動名詞片語，故代名詞用 it，選 (D) *is it*。
      * *get up* 起床   early〔ˋɝlɪ〕*adv.* 早

4.(**A**) 今天晚上我會待在辦公室直到我<u>完成</u>工作。

      表時間或條件的副詞子句，須用現在式代替未來式，故選 (A)
      finish〔ˋfɪnɪʃ〕*v.* 完成。
      * office〔ˋɔfɪs〕*n.* 辦公室   work〔wɝk〕*n.* 工作

5.(**B**) 查爾斯在百貨公司<u>花了</u>一天的時間為他的太太尋找一頂帽子。

      (A) cost〔kɔst〕*v.*（事物）花費（金錢）

(B) ***spend***〔spɛnd〕*v.*（人）花費（時間、金錢）

(C) see〔si〕*v.* 看見　　　(D) make〔mek〕*v.* 做

* ***department store*** 百貨公司　　***look for*** 尋找

6.**(B)**　湯姆在過去兩個月內<u>已經減掉</u>十磅。他現在看起來瘦多了。

依句意，須用現在完成式，表從過去到現在已完的動作，故選

(B) ***has lost***。lose〔luz〕*v.* 減輕【lost 為過去分詞】

* pound〔paʊnd〕*n.* 磅　　　thin〔θɪn〕*adj.* 瘦的

7.**(D)**　我不喜歡這三支手錶的任何一支。你可以給我看<u>另一個</u>嗎？

(A) the others　其餘的人或物

(B) other〔ˈʌðɚ〕*adj.* 其他的

(C) either〔ˈiðɚ〕*adj.* 兩者之一的

(D) ***another***〔əˈnʌðɚ〕*adj.* 另一個的

* show〔ʃo〕*v.* 給…看

8.**(B)**　服務生被要求要<u>有禮貌</u>；他們應該總是要微笑，並且記得說「歡迎光臨」和「請」。

(A) honest〔ˈɑnɪst〕*adj.* 誠實的

(B) ***polite***〔pəˈlaɪt〕*adj.* 有禮貌的

(C) special〔ˈspɛʃəl〕*adj.* 特別的

(D) strong〔strɔŋ〕*adj.* 強壯的

* waiter〔ˈwetɚ〕*n.* 服務生　　　ask〔æsk〕*v.* 要求

welcome〔ˈwɛlkəm〕*interj.* 歡迎光臨；歡迎

9.**(D)**　在兒童節的時候，李女士，一位有名的童話書作家，<u>會來到</u>茉莉書店談論她的新書。我的兩個小孩真的等不及要見她。

依句意，應用未來式，可用「will + 原形 V.」或「be going to + V.」，故選 (D) ***is going to come***。

* ***Children's Day*** 兒童節　　　famous〔ˈfeməs〕*adj.* 有名的

storybook〔ˈstorɪˌbʊk〕*n.* 童話書；故事書

writer〔ˈraɪtɚ〕*n.* 作家　　　bookstore〔ˈbʊkˌstor〕*n.* 書店

just〔dʒʌst〕*adv.* 真地；完全

10.(**D**) 沒有人認為詹姆士會出現在凱蒂的派對上。所以當他<u>出現</u>的時候，每個人都很驚訝，不敢相信他們的眼睛。

> 依句意為過去式，故選 (D) **did**，代替過去分詞 appeared。
>
> * appear〔ə'pɪr〕v. 出現　　surprised〔sə'praɪzd〕adj. 驚訝的

11.(**B**) B&J 咖啡廳<u>以</u>鎮上最高的建築物<u>聞名</u>。然而，O&G 餐廳在 2010 年成為最高的建築物。

> 依句意，「B&J 咖啡廳是最高的建築物」是過去一段時間的事，故用「過去完成式」，選 (B) **had been**。
>
> * **be known as** 以…聞名　　building〔'bɪldɪŋ〕n. 建築物
> become〔bɪ'kʌm〕v. 成為

12.(**D**) 在被訪問許多次之後，<u>因</u>這部電影<u>而著名</u>的演員大衛・派普變得厭倦於談論它。

> 依句意，選 (D) **he is famous for**。
>
> **be famous for** 「他…而著名。」
>
> * actor〔'æktɚ〕n. 演員　　tired〔taɪrd〕adj. 厭倦的 < of >
> **talk about** 談論　　interview〔'ɪntɚ,vju〕v. 訪問；訪談
> time〔taɪm〕n. 次數

第二部分：題組（第 13-40 題，共 28 題）

（13～15）

從：莉莎・克萊

致：瑪莉・菲柏

日期：2015 年 4 月 2 日，星期四

主旨：歡迎

- -

親愛的瑪莉：

比利叔叔和我對妳的造訪感到很興奮。

這幾天天氣<u>變化很大</u>。像今天，早上是晴天，但是中午的時候下大
　　　　　　13

雨。所以我們已<u>經替妳擬定了兩個計劃</u>：如果是好天氣，我會帶妳
　　　　　　　　　　14

去史密斯農場。他們這週有特別的馬術表演。我確定妳會喜歡它。

<u>如果下雨也別擔心</u>。我們可以去咪咪百貨公司購物；我們可在那邊
　　　　15

到處走走，不會被淋濕。不論晴雨，我們希望妳在這裡玩得愉快。

明天早上九點火車站見。

愛妳的，
莉莎阿姨

【註釋】

subject〔ˈsʌbdʒɪkt〕*n.* 主旨　　visit〔ˈvɪzɪt〕*n.* 造訪；拜訪
weather〔ˈwɛðɚ〕*n.* 天氣　　sunny〔ˈsʌnɪ〕*adj.* 晴朗的
heavily〔ˈhɛvɪlɪ〕*adv.* 猛烈地　　noon〔nun〕*n.* 正午
farm〔fɑrm〕*n.* 農場　　have〔hæv〕*v.* 舉行　　show〔ʃo〕*n.* 表演
sure〔ʃur〕*adj.* 確定的　　***walk around*** 四處走動
wet〔wɛt〕*adj.* 濕的　　shine〔ʃaɪn〕*n.* 晴天
rain or shine 不論晴雨　　hope〔hop〕*v.* 希望
have a good time 玩得愉快　　***train station*** 火車站

13. (**C**) (A) 好轉 　　　　　　　(B) 很溫暖
　　　　　　(C) <u>變化很大</u>　　　　　 (D) 變得又濕又冷
　　　　　　* change〔tʃendʒ〕*v.* 改變　　***a lot*** 很多；常常

14. (**A**) (A) <u>替妳擬定了兩個計劃</u>　　(B) 擔心妳到這裡的旅程
　　　　　　(C) 決定帶妳去一個好地方　　(D) 準備妳所求的一切
　　　　　　* ***worry about*** 擔心　　trip〔trɪp〕*n.* 旅行
　　　　　　decide〔dɪˈsaɪd〕*v.* 決定

15. (**B**) (A) 我們會和諧相處　　　　(B) 如果下雨也不用擔心
　　　　　(C) 我們都很愛動物　　　　(D) 不要忘了看一下天氣

　　* agree〔ə'gri〕v. 同意；和諧相處 < with >
　　　animal〔'ænəmḷ〕n. 動物　　　check〔tʃɛk〕v. 查看

(16～18)

新聞追追追

基蘭‧哈迪 11/07/2013

　　多年來，我們認為地球是那裡唯一的一個藍點。現在，有另一個被找到了。它的名字是 HD18973b。HD18973b 是一個系外行星，在我們的太陽系之外，而且是最接近地球的其中一個。即便如此，我們無法真的稱它為鄰居。原因是：它距離我們有 63 光年遠。那
　　　　　　　16
意味著它離我們有 370,440,000,000,000 英里遠。即使我們每小時飛行 3,500 公里，也將要花超過一千兩百萬年才能到達那裡。

　　除了是藍色的，HD18973b 完全不像我們的地球：它比地球大
　　　　　　　　　　　　17
得多，由氣體所組成，而且非常酷熱。在高達攝氏 1,000 度的熱度下，是不可能有生命的。更糟的是，它下玻璃雨。如果攝氏 1,000度殺不死你，玻璃雨也會。

　　雖然如此，找到這個藍色巨人給了我們希望。這是第一次我
　　　　　　　　　　　　　　　18
們能夠看到系外行星的顏色。行星的顏色讓我們知道該行星上面發生什麼事。雖然在我們找到可居住的新星球前，還有很長的一段路要走，但找到一個藍點是一個好的開始。

【註釋】

news〔njuz〕*n.* 新聞　　hunt〔hʌnt〕*n.* 追蹤

Earth〔ɝθ〕*n.* 地球　　dot〔dɑt〕*n.* 點；小點

outside〔aʊtˈsaɪd〕*prep.* 在…之外　　*up there* 在那裡

exoplanet〔ˈɛksəˌplænɪt〕*n.* 系外行星

solar〔ˈsolɚ〕*adj.* 太陽的　　system〔ˈsɪstəm〕*n.* 系統

Solar System 太陽系　　*even so* 即使如此（= *however*）

light year 光年【距離單位】　　mean〔min〕*v.* 意思是

mile〔maɪl〕*n.* 英里【1.6 公里】　　*even if* 即使

fly〔flaɪ〕*v.* 飛；飛行　　take〔tek〕*v.* 花費（時間）

million〔ˈmɪljən〕*adj.* 百萬的　　get〔gɛt〕*v.* 到達

much〔mʌtʃ〕*adv.*【修飾比較級】大大地；非常

be made of 由…製成　　gas〔gæs〕*n.* 氣體

burning〔ˈbɝnɪŋ〕*adv.* 如火燒地　　*burning hot* 酷熱

heat〔hit〕*n.* 熱度；溫度　　～°*C* 攝氏～度（= *degree Celsius*）

life〔laɪf〕*n.* 生命　　possible〔ˈpɑsəbḷ〕*adj.* 可能的

what is worse 更糟的是（= *to make matters worse*）

rain〔ren〕*v.* 使…如雨般降落　　glass〔glæs〕*n.* 玻璃狀的東西

kill〔kɪl〕*v.* 殺死；使喪生　　giant〔ˈdʒaɪənt〕*n.* 巨人；巨大的東西

the first time 第一次　　*be able to V.* 能夠～

color〔ˈkʌlɚ〕*n.* 顏色　　idea〔aɪˈdiə〕*n.* 概念；知識

while〔hwaɪl〕*conj.* 雖然（= *though*）

way〔we〕*n.* 路程　　start〔stɑrt〕*n.* 開始

16. (**A**) (A) 我們無法真的稱它為鄰居

　　　(B) 我們對它還一無所知

　　　(C) 我們可能無法在那裡待很久

　　　(D) 我們無法確定要花多久時間才能到達那裡

　　　* call〔kɔl〕*v.* 稱…（為）　　neighbor〔ˈnebɚ〕*n.* 鄰居

　　　yet〔jɛt〕*adv.* 尚（未）；還（沒）　　*for long* 長久地

17. (**C**) (A) 此外，並不是水讓 HD18973b 看起來是藍色的

(B) 藍色的 HD18973b 可能會是我們另一個地球

(C) <u>除了是藍色的，HD18973b 完全不像我們的地球</u>

(D) 因為它的藍色，人們猜想 HD18973b 上可能有生命存在

* ***what's more*** 此外（= *moreover*）

a second 另一個（= *another*）

except for 除了⋯之外　　***be nothing like*** 完全不像

planet〔ˈplænɪt〕*n.* 行星　　***home planet*** 地球（= *earth*）

because of 因為　　guess〔gɛs〕*v.* 猜測

18. (**A**) (A) <u>給我們希望</u>　　　　　　(B) 需要很努力

(C) 已經改變了我們的生活　　(D) 幫助我們更了解地球

* take〔tek〕*v.* 需要　　***hard work*** 努力　　help〔hɛlp〕*v.* 幫助

（ 19 ~ 20 ）

　　　　上週六，吉妮和她的朋友在霍爾的碗吃午餐。這裡是他們點的餐點，以及餐廳的海報。

霍 爾 的 碗			
桌號 *2*	*3* 人	點餐人員：佛瑞德	*12:30 12/23*
1	南瓜派		220×2
2	起司蛋糕		120×1
3	奶昔（巧克力）（大）		200×2
4	奶昔（香蕉）		110×1
5	雞肉三明治		100×1
6	雞肉三明治（加起司）		120×1
7	可樂（去冰）		65×1
8	柳橙汁（去冰）		90×1
9	葡萄汁		95×1
10			
		總價：$1,540	
謝謝您並希望很快再次見到您!!　電話：XXX-XXX			

霍 爾 的 碗

營業時間：
11:30am-11:30pm
週二到週日

歡樂時光：八折
下午2:00-4:00
晚上9:30-11:30

【註釋】

bowl〔bol〕*n.* 碗　　order〔ˋɔrdɚ〕*n.* 點餐

poster〔ˋpostɚ〕*n.* 海報　　restaurant〔ˋrɛstərənt〕*n.* 餐廳

take** one's **order 接受點菜　　pumpkin〔ˋpʌmpkɪn〕*n.* 南瓜

pie〔paɪ〕*n.* 派　　cheese〔tʃiz〕*n.* 起司　　***milk shake*** 奶昔

chocolate〔ˋtʃɔkəlɪt〕*n.* 巧克力　　sandwich〔ˋsændwɪtʃ〕*n.* 三明治

cola〔ˋkolə〕*n.* 可樂　　***orange juice*** 柳橙汁

grape〔grep〕*n.* 葡萄　　total〔ˋtotl̩〕*adj.* 總共的；全部的

hours〔aʊrz〕*n. pl.* 時間　　***open hours*** 營業時間

joy〔dʒɔɪ〕*n.* 快樂　　off〔ɔf〕*adv.* （減）掉；（扣）掉

20% off 打八折　　***am*** 上午（= *a.m.*）　　***pm*** 下午（= *p.m.*）

19.（ **B** ）在點菜單上，吉妮點了一個加起司的三明治，一杯水果奶昔，和
　　　　一個去冰的水果飲料。她需要為她的食物付多少錢？

　　　　(A) $300。　　(B) $320。　　(C) $385。　　(D) $410。

　　　　* list〔lɪst〕*n.* 表；價目表　　pay〔pe〕*v.* 支付< *for* >

20.（ **D** ）吉妮想要在歡樂時光的時候再去霍爾的碗。她可能何時會去？

　　　　(A) 星期三早上 11:00。　　　　(B) 星期一下午 2:30。

　　　　(C) 星期五晚上 8:30。　　　　(D) 星期四晚上 10:00。

（21～23）

以下是四個學生在課堂上如何回答老師的問題。

莉莉：我喜歡購物和與人交談。我覺得我可以學習如何做生
　　　意。也許賣衣服對我來說是一門好生意。

雷恩：我的嗜好是打電動遊戲和網路交友。我們常常藉由電子
　　　郵件分享我們有趣的故事。我想我會多了解電腦，然後
　　　做出超級聰明的電腦程式。

比利：我的父母從我小的時候就已經養很多的寵物。我們已經一起經歷了很多事情，好的和壞的，快樂的和悲傷的。那些事情永遠在我的腦海裡。有一天，我會把<u>它們</u>經由圖畫和寫書與人分享。

安娜：雖然我媽媽和兩個姐姐都是醫生，但我肯定我會盡我所能地遠離醫院。我討厭生病，而且我害怕看到病人看起來虛弱和悲傷的樣子。我會每天做我最喜歡的運動——打網球，保持強壯。有一天我會加入國家隊，並成爲另一個盧彥勳。

【註釋】

below〔bə'lo〕adv. 在下方　　**in class** 在課堂上
shopping〔'ʃɑpɪŋ〕n. 購物　　**do business** 做生意
maybe〔'mebɪ〕adv. 或許（= *perhaps*）
hobby〔'hɑbɪ〕n. 嗜好　　**computer game** 電腦遊戲
make friends 交朋友　　online〔'ɑn,laɪn〕adv. 在網路上
share〔ʃɛr〕v. 分享　　funny〔'fʌnɪ〕adj. 好笑的
e-mail〔'i,mel〕n. 電子郵件
super-smart〔'supɚ,smɑrt〕adj. 超級聰明的
program〔'progræm〕n. 程式　　pet〔pɛt〕n. 寵物
keep a pet 養寵物　　experience〔ɪk'spɪrɪəns〕v. 經歷
in one's **mind** 在某人的腦海中
one day 有一天（= *some day*）
draw〔drɔ〕v. 畫　　**stay far away from** 遠離
as…**as one can** 儘可能　　sick〔sɪk〕adj. 生病的
be afraid of 害怕　　weak〔wik〕adj. 虛弱的
strong〔strɔŋ〕adj. 強壯的；強健的
favorite〔'fevərɪt〕adj. 最喜愛的　　tennis〔'tɛnɪs〕n. 網球
join〔dʒɔɪn〕v. 加入　　**national team** 國家代表隊

21.（ **A** ） 老師很可能在課堂上問了什麼問題？

　　　　(A) 「你未來想做什麼？」

　　　　(B) 「對即將到來的假期你有什麼計畫？」

　　　　(C) 「你喜歡和你的朋友談論些什麼？」

　　　　(D) 「你最喜歡和你的家人一起做什麼？」

　　　　* *most likely* 很可能（ = *very likely* ）

　　　　in the future 在未來；將來

　　　　coming〔ˈkʌmɪŋ〕 *adj.* 即將到來的

　　　　vacation〔veˈkeʃən〕 *n.* 假期

22.（ **C** ） 從本文中我們可以得知什麼？

　　　　(A) 莉莉擅長做衣服。　　(B) 比爾的父母其中一人是獸醫。

　　　　(C) 雷恩喜歡在網路上認識人。

　　　　(D) 安娜曾經生重病而且在醫院待了很長的一段時間。

　　　　* *be good at* 擅長於　　　*animal doctor* 獸醫（ = *vet* ）

　　　　meet〔mit〕 *v.* 認識　　Internet〔ˈɪntəˌnɛt〕 *n.* 網際網路

　　　　once〔wʌns〕 *adv.* 曾經

23.（ **C** ） them 是什麼意思？

　　　　(A) 寵物。　　(B) 書籍。　　(C) 故事。　　(D) 父母。

（ 24～25 ）

　這是尼克・佛斯特的新書《嫁給食物》的序言。

序　言

　　我的母親很不會做菜。對她來說，烹飪是比較像是令人興奮的實驗。你把一些這個和一些那個放在鍋子裡，然後等著看會發生什麼事。「沒有實驗，就沒有經驗」是當她的實驗結果並不好時，她會說的話，而且我聽過很多遍。

> 我的父親很會做菜,而且他也愛做菜。他經常說,他是以一桌美味的食物讓我的母親嫁給他,而不是用一個美麗的戒指。他說:「一個家庭只需要一個好廚師。」
>
> 現在我自己是位廚師。而且我有自己的餐廳。當然,我從我父親那學會了如何烹飪。從他身上,我學到了烹飪的藝術。但我確實從我母親那學到了一件事,那就是她的一句名言:「沒有實驗,就沒有經驗。」

【註釋】

perface〔'prefɪs〕*n.* 前言;序言　　lousy〔'lauzɪ〕*adj.* 糟糕的;差勁的
exciting〔ɪk'saɪtɪŋ〕*adj.* 令人興奮的
experiment〔ɪk'spɛrəmənt〕*n.* 實驗　　pot〔pɑt〕*n.* 鍋子
wait and see 等著瞧　　experience〔ɪk'spɪrɪəns〕*n.* 經驗
turn out 結果成為　　***a lot*** 常常　　cook〔kuk〕*n.* 廚師　*v.* 煮菜
get〔gɛt〕*v.* 使　　marry〔'mærɪ〕*v.* 娶;嫁
delicious〔dɪ'lɪʃəs〕*adj.* 美味的　　ring〔rɪŋ〕*n.* 戒指
own〔on〕*adj.* 自己的　　***of course*** 當然　　art〔ɑrt〕*n.* 藝術
saying〔'seɪŋ〕*n.* 話;名言;諺語

24. (**B**) 當某人 <u>lousy at</u> 某事時,是什麼意思?
　　(A) 他們因此而有名。　　　　(B) <u>他們無法做好。</u>
　　(C) 他們認為它很重要。　　　(D) 他們對它不感興趣。
　　* ***be interested in*** 對⋯感興趣

25. (**C**) 我們從序言可得知什麼?
　　(A) 佛斯特如何創立他自己的餐廳。
　　(B) 佛斯特的父親何時娶了他的母親。
　　(C) <u>關於烹飪,佛斯特的母親教了他什麼。</u>
　　(D) 佛斯特如何從他父親身上學到烹飪的藝術。
　　* learn〔lɝn〕*n.* 知道　　start〔stɑrt〕*v.* 創立

（26～27）

以下是一個叫作「旅行到夢幻世界」遊戲的規則。

1. 每一個玩家都在**起始點**開始。
2. 每一回合，要先抽四張牌 🌙 ❄ ☼ 💧 裡的一張，來決定要移動幾步：🌙 代表一步，❄ 代表兩步，☼ 代表三步，💧 代表移動四步。然後，如果有 👉 在你所到達的地方，就要遵守 👉 旁的指示，
3. 第一個到達夢幻世界的人，就贏得這局比賽。

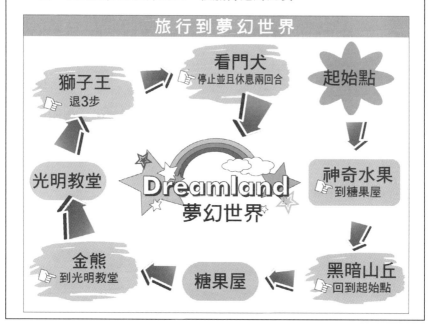

【註釋】

rule〔rul〕*n.* 規則　　game〔gem〕*n.* 遊戲；比賽

call〔kɔl〕*v.* 稱為　　dreamland〔'drim,lænd〕*n.* 夢境；夢幻世界

player〔'pleɚ〕*n.* 遊戲的人　　begin〔bɪ'gɪn〕*v.* 開始

start〔trɪp〕*n.* 出發點　*v.* 開始　　turn〔tɜn〕*n.* 回合
first〔fɜst〕*adv.* 首先　　card〔kard〕*n.* 撲克牌
space〔spes〕*n.* 步；格　　move〔muv〕*v.* 移動
follow〔'falo〕*v.* 遵照　　word〔wɜd〕*n.* 字
next to 在…旁邊　　arrive〔ə'raɪv〕*v.* 到達
get to 到達　　win〔wɪn〕*v.* 贏
magic〔'mædʒɪk〕*adj.* 魔法的；不可思議的
dark〔dɑrk〕*adj.* 暗的　　hill〔hɪl〕*n.* 山丘
golden〔'goldn̩〕*adj.* 金色的　　bear〔bɛr〕*n.* 熊
light〔laɪt〕*adj.* 光明的　　church〔tʃɜtʃ〕*n.* 教堂
lion〔'laɪən〕*n.* 獅子　　gate〔get〕*n.* 大門
watchdog〔'watʃ,dɔg〕*n.* 看門狗

26. (**C**) 下列是四個小孩開始玩遊戲之後，他們所拿到的牌。誰贏得這場
比賽？

27. (**A**) 我們可以從這場遊戲得知什麼？

(A) <u>沒有人可以從獅子王開始玩遊戲。</u>

(B) 卡牌可以決定誰先開始玩。

(C) 沒有人可以在第一回合就到達光明教堂。

(D) 卡牌可以決定從哪裡開始遊戲。

(28～31)

　　你可能每年會有一兩次<u>這樣的想法</u>。在一個炎熱的夏日，你
回到家，希望可以洗個冷水澡，卻發現沒有水。然後你才了解到
水在你的日常生活中有多重要。然而，在世界上很多地方，水並
不僅僅是人們的日常需求而已。

　　在像坦尚尼亞這種國家，水很難取得，而取水這樣重要的工作，就落到了女人的肩上。當男孩們在學校唸書時，女孩們常常被迫留在家中來收集水。研究顯示，住在距離乾淨水源處僅 15 分鐘路程的坦尚尼亞的女孩，比起距離 1 小時路程的女孩，能夠獲得多 12%的學校學習時間。花更多的時間收集水，就代表了更少的學習時間。對這些女孩來說，「知識就是力量」這句話，並不僅僅是一句話；這是她們真實生活中一項悲哀的事實。由於她們上學的時間減少，未來要得到高薪的工作的機會就更小，也因此沒有權利在重要事情上發聲，譬如她們的婚姻對象。這些女孩常常得嫁入貧窮的家庭裡。她們沒有什麼錢或知識來照顧她們的小孩，而這些小孩常常年紀輕輕就去世了。對於那些僥倖存活下來的女孩，她們的命運可能仍然是以「水」為中心，就像她們的母親一樣。

【註釋】

hit〔hɪt〕*v.* 使突然想起　　once〔wʌns〕*adv.* 一次
twice〔twaɪs〕*adv.* 兩次　　*have a bath* 洗澡
cool〔kul〕*adj.* 涼爽的　　*find out* 發現　　see〔si〕*v.* 知道
important〔ɪm'pɔrtn̩t〕*adj.* 重要的　　*everyday life* 日常生活
however〔hau'ɛvɚ〕*adv.* 然而　　part〔part〕*n.* 部份
country〔'kʌntrɪ〕*n.* 國家　　like〔laɪk〕*prep.* 像
Tanzania〔tænzə'niə〕*n.* 坦尚尼亞（位於非洲中東部）
hard〔hard〕*adj.* 困難的　　collect〔kə'lɛkt〕*v.* 收集
fall on 落在…上　　shoulder〔'ʃoldɚ〕*n.* 肩膀
keep〔kip〕*v.* 使停留
be kept home from school 被留在家，不能去上學
studies〔'stʌdɪz〕*n. pl.* 研究　　spend〔spɛnd〕*v.* 花費；度過（時間）
away〔ə'we〕*adv.* 在（某距離）以外
knowledge〔'nɑlɪdʒ〕*n.* 知識　　power〔'pauɚ〕*n.* 力量
real〔'riəl〕*adj.* 現實的　　chances〔'tʃænsɪz〕*n. pl.* 希望；可能性

well-paid〔͵wɛl'ped〕*adj.* 高薪的
voice〔vɔɪs〕*n.* 聲音；發言權；意見　　marry〔'mærɪ〕*v.* 和…結婚
be married into 嫁入　　***take care of*** 照顧
end up + V-ing 最後~　　***die young*** 早死；夭折
center around 以…為中心

28.(**A**) 在本文中，<u>The idea</u>是什麼意思？

(A) <u>水在人們的日常生活中很重要。</u>

(B) 水並不只與人們的日常生活需求有關而已。

(C) 在炎熱的夏天裡，洗個冷水澡是很棒的。

(D) 我們不該在沒什麼水的時候洗澡。

* little〔'lɪtl̩〕*adj.* 很少的

29.(**C**) 本文的主旨為何？

(A) 為何省水是重要的。

(B) 水是如何給予一個國家力量的。

(C) <u>水可能會如何影響一個人的未來。</u>

(D) 在貧窮國家，為什麼水很難取得。

* save〔sev〕*v.* 節省
play a part 扮演一個角色；在…方面起作用

30.(**B**) 我們可從本文得知什麼？

(A) 在貧窮的國家裡，孩子們常死於飲用不乾淨的水。

(B) <u>沒時間上學的女孩，在長大後常常過著較辛苦的生活。</u>

(C) 在像坦尚尼亞這種國家的女孩，做同樣工作的收入低於男孩。

(D) 困苦家庭的小孩常因要照顧更年幼的孩子而無法上學。

* ***die from*** 因…而死　　***grow up*** 長大
same〔sem〕*adj.* 同樣的

31.(**D**)　在貝南、迦納、幾內亞、以及馬達加斯加這些國家的家庭，和坦尚尼亞的家庭一樣，都要處理集水的工作。從本文可知，下列哪個圖表最能反映出這個狀況？

(A)
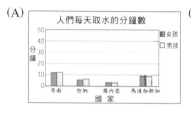

(B)
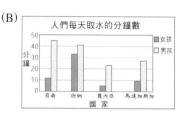

(C)
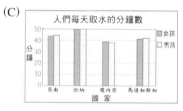

(D)
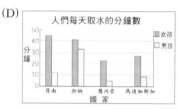

＊ Benin〔ˊbɛnɪn〕*n.* 貝南（非洲西部一共和國）
　Ghana〔ˊgɑnə〕*n.* 迦納（西非國家）
　Guinea〔ˊgɪnɪ〕*n.* 幾內亞（西非國家）
　Madagascar〔͵mædəˊgæskɚ〕*n.* 馬達加斯加

（ 32～34 ）

（在麗茲的生日宴會上）

安珀：別告訴我你沒有去「花園小屋」。

契斯：我為何要去那裡？

安珀：為了麗茲的生日蛋糕呀！我今天早上有留語音留言給
　　　你！

契斯：但是妳說麥特會去麵包店！而且，妳為什麼沒有等我就
　　　來這裡？我在妳公寓外面等了一個小時！

> 安珀：不！我說我會跟麥特一起吃午餐，然後我們會從餐廳直
> 接來這裡。所以我要你下班後幫我拿蛋糕。
>
> 契斯：不，妳沒有！而且妳為什麼不接我的電話？
>
> 安珀：我的手機沒電了！我在訊息裡說，如果你想找我的話，
> 你可以打麥特的電話。現在請你告訴我，你有帶我們買
> 給麗茲的禮物。
>
> 契斯：什麼禮物？我很確定妳在訊息中根本沒提到禮物。
>
> 安珀：我昨天就告訴你了！

【註釋】

garden〔'gɑrdn̩〕*n.* 花園　　***voice message*** 語音留言
bakery〔'bekərɪ〕*n.* 麵包店　　apartment〔ə'pɑrtmənt〕*n.* 公寓
have lunch 吃午餐　　straight〔stret〕*adv.* 直接地
after work 下班後　　***answer*** one's ***call*** 接某人的電話
cellphone〔'sɛl,fon〕*n.* 手機（= cell phone）
dead〔dɛd〕*adj.* 沒電的　　***call*** one's ***number*** 打某人的電話號碼
gift〔gɪft〕*n.* 禮物

32.（**A**）「花園小屋」是什麼？

　　(A) 一間麵包店。　　　(B) 一間禮品店。

　　(C) 一間花店。　　　　(D) 一間公寓。

33.（**C**）關於契斯，我們可以知道什麼事？

　　(A) 他忘了和安珀和及麥特見面吃午餐。

　　(B) 他不知道如何去安珀的公寓。

　　(C) 他在不知道安珀的手機不能用的情況下，打了電話給她。

　　(D) 他不知道安珀今天早上留了個語音留言給他。

　　* meet〔mit〕*v.* 和…見面　　work〔wɜk〕*v.* 運作

34. (**A**) 哪個句子最有可能是來自於安珀今天早上留給契斯的訊息？

　　(A) 「麥特跟我將會在午餐後去參加派對。」

　　(B) 「別忘了買給麗茲的生日禮物。」

　　(C) 「你可以直接從你的辦公室去參加派對。」

　　(D) 「這個週末，我需要與你討論一下這個派對。」

　　* weekend〔'wik'ɛnd〕*n.* 週末

(35～36)

　　　　小蛙是隻從來不記得自己去過哪裡的青蛙。他最大的夢想就是找到一個最棒的池溏，可以讓他不用擔心水蛇，自在地游來游去。有一天，小蛙蹦蹦跳跳地進入廚房，並跳入了一個裝滿熱水的鍋子中。他感到熾熱的高溫，牠以最快的速度急忙跳出熱水。「我差點就死在那裡了！」小蛙心想。

　　　　幾天後，小蛙回到了同一個廚房，完全忘了自己曾經去過那裡。他再次跳入的相同的鍋子裡。這一次，裡面的水是涼的。牠環顧四周後，心想：「這裡沒有要吃我的水蛇，而且我可以獨自使用這個地方！」牠這時候了解到，這就是牠夢想中的池塘。而他所不知道的是，水正在用小火加溫。

　　　　游了三十分鐘後，小蛙覺得水比較溫暖了，但牠覺得這是個不錯的驚喜。「這裡真是個最適合游泳的地方。我也要來洗個熱水澡。」在他洗澡洗得很舒服時，水變得越來越熱。小蛙因為太舒服而睡著了。而從此牠就再也沒醒來過了。

【註釋】

frog〔frɑg〕*n.* 青蛙　　***have been*** 曾經去過　　pond〔pɑnd〕*n.* 池溏
freely〔'frilɪ〕*adv.* 自在地　　snake〔snek〕*n.* 蛇
water snake 水蛇　　hop〔hɑp〕*v.* 跳　　jump〔dʒʌmp〕*v.* 跳
full of … 充滿了…的　　heat〔hit〕*n.* 熱度
hurry〔'hɜɪ〕*v.* 匆忙（做…）　　carry〔'kærɪ〕*v.* 攜帶；支撐
as fast as *one's* ***legs can carry*** *one* 以最快的速度；以全速
die〔daɪ〕*v.* 死　　totally〔'totl̩ɪ〕*adv.* 完全　　***this time*** 這一次
inside〔'ɪn,saɪd〕*adv.* 在裡面　　***look around*** 環顧四周
to oneself 獨自地　　***at that moment*** 在那個時候
dream〔drim〕*adj.* 夢想的　　***warm up*** 加熱　　***a low heat*** 小火
think of A as B 認為 A 是 B　　surprise〔sə'praɪs〕*n.* 令人驚訝的事
get to 得以　　comfortable〔'kʌmfətəbl̩〕*adj.* 舒服的
get warmer and warmer 變得越來越溫暖　　***fall asleep*** 睡著

35.(**C**) 我們可以從小蛙的故事中學到什麼教訓？

　　(A) 生命太短暫，我們要過最充實的生活。

　　(B) 善用時間的人到最後會成為贏家。

　　(C) 人們對逐漸惡化的問題常視而不見。

　　(D) 改掉舊習慣很困難，但養成新的習慣卻很簡單。

　　* lesson〔'lɛsn̩〕*n.* 教訓　　full〔ful〕*adj.* 滿的；最高限度的
　　to the full 完全地；充分地
　　live life to the fullest 要讓生活儘量充實　　***in the end*** 最後
　　get worse 變糟；惡化　　***over time*** 隨著時間的過去
　　give up 放棄；戒除（習慣）　　***pick up*** 學會；獲得

36.(**B**) 關於小蛙，我們知道些什麼？

　　(A) 牠學到跟他人分享自己喜歡的東西。

　　(B) 牠以為牠的心願已經成真。

　　(C) 牠曾經幾乎因為水蛇而失去親密的朋友。

　　(D) 牠想要回到相同的鍋子洗熱水澡。

　　* ***hope for*** 期待；希望　　***become real*** 成真
　　lose *sth.* ***to*** *sb.* 被某人奪去某物　　dear〔dɪr〕*adj.* 親愛的

（37～40）

大都會日報
2020 年 10 月 1 日

　　這些年來教會的處境堪憂。首先，上教堂的人數銳減（見表一）。很多人說他們不屬於任何教會，而那些教友們則是比以往更少上教堂。上教堂這件事越來越少出現在人們的待辦清單上。另一個令人擔心的事情是，越來越少年輕人上教堂，導致教堂的老年化（見表二）。

　　再來，財務上也出現問題。經營教堂所費不貲。越少人上教堂，就表示金錢的收入越少。這使得經營教堂更不容易。

　　當教堂面臨關閉時，往往除了賣掉之外，沒有什麼辦法。那些幸運能找到買主的教堂，會被移作他用。例如，有些被改成餐廳或學校體育館，而有些甚至變成夜店。有些不幸的教堂最後被拆除。

　　就像是一間一直生意減少的商店，必須要想辦法挽救自己一樣，或許現在正是教堂要試著贏回人心，並且重新在人們的生活中，扮演重要角色的時候了。這不是只要單純祈禱就能得到答案的。

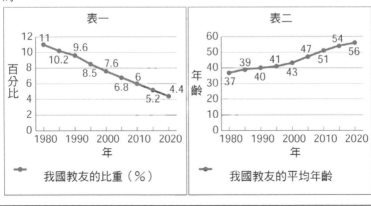

【註釋】

church〔tʃɜtʃ〕*n.* 教堂；教會

calamitous〔kə'læmətəs〕*adj.* 悲慘的　　state〔stet〕*n.* 狀態

to start with 首先　　church-goer　*n.* 上教堂的人；教友

drop〔drɑp〕*v.* 下降　　sharply〔'ʃɑrplɪ〕*adv.* 急劇地

figure〔'fɪgjɚ〕*n.* 圖表；數字

many〔'mɛnɪ〕*pron.* 很多人（= *many people*）

belong to 屬於　　***those who***… 那些…的人　　***used to*** 以前

go to church 上教堂；做禮拜　　appear〔ə'pɪr〕*v.* 似乎；出現

less and less 越來越少　　***to-do list*** 待辦清單

worrying〔'wɜɪɪŋ〕*adj.* 令人擔憂的　　***fewer and fewer*** 越來越少的

lead to 導致　　***come in***（錢）進帳；收入

There is little to do but to V. 除了…之外，沒什麼辦法。

lucky〔'lʌkɪ〕*adj.* 幸運　　***be put to other uses*** 被移作他用

gym〔dʒɪm〕*n.* 體育館　　nightclub〔'naɪt,klʌb〕*n.* 夜店

knock down 拆毀　　***in the end*** 到最後　　***lose business*** 失去生意

save〔sev〕*v.* 拯救　　***think of*** 想到　　***win back*** 贏回

play an important part 擔任重要角色（= *play an important role*）

pray〔pre〕*v.* 祈禱；禱告　　percentage〔pɚ'sɛntɪdʒ〕*n.* 百分比

average〔'ævərɪdʒ〕*adj.* 平均的

37. (**A**) 當某人<u>處境堪憂</u>時，是什麼意思？

　　(A) <u>他們有嚴重的問題。</u>　　(B) 他們試著改變自己。

　　(C) 他們在找另一個機會。

　　(D) 他們對外面的世界沒有興趣。

　　* serious〔'sɪrɪəs〕*adj.* 嚴重的　　***look for*** 尋找

　　　interest〔'ɪntrɪst〕*n.* 興趣　　***outside world*** 外界

38. (**C**) 我們從報導中，可以得知關於教友的什麼事？

　　(A) 在 1980 到 2005 年間，很少教友小於五十歲。

　　(B) 在 2010 年時，只有百分之六的教友小於五十歲。

　　(C) <u>在 2020 年時，教友的百分比下降到比 1980 年的一半還少。</u>

　　(D) 在 1980 到 2020 年間，老教友的人數上升，導致教會老年化。

* report〔rɪˋport〕*n.* 報導

　lower〔ˋloɚ〕*adj.* 較低的【low 的比較級】

　half〔hæf〕*adj.* …的一半的　　　　rising〔ˋraɪzɪŋ〕*adj.* 上升的

39. (**C**)　報導中談論了什麼？

　　(A) 教會的財務流向。　　　　(B) 人們如何決定加入教會。

　　(C) 關門的教堂發生什麼事。　(D) 人們不再上教堂的原因。

　　* *stop* + *V-ing* 停止做~

40. (**D**)　以下是來自其他報導的四項發現。哪一項和本報導的想法不一致？

　　(A) 「報告顯示，超過百分之九十的教友會上教堂，因為他們
　　　　的父親會去。在過去的二十年，小於三十歲的男性中，有
　　　　百分之四十九的人離開教堂。那意味著有九成的機會，他
　　　　們的小孩不會上教堂。這對教堂來說，是難以接受的。」

　　(B) 「在 2003 到 2010 年間，全國建立了超過 1,000 間新的教
　　　　堂。那可能聽起來是個好消息。然而，在同樣這些年間，
　　　　有超過二千間教堂關閉。」

　　(C) 「在該報導裡，百分之三十三受訪的人說，他們從不上教
　　　　堂，而另外百分之三十三的人說，他們以前會去。只有百
　　　　分之十五的人，一個月至少上一次教堂。」

　　(D) 「在報導中的十五個國家裡，某些國家教友的百分比，像
　　　　是丹麥，是低於百分之十；在其他國家，像是波蘭，百分
　　　　比高於百分之七十。」

　　* findings〔ˋfaɪndɪŋz〕*n. pl.* 發現的東西；調查的結果

　　　agree with 和…一致　　　show〔ʃo〕*v.* 顯示

　　　last〔læst〕*adj.* 過去的　　*take in* 接受（= *accept*）

　　　build〔bɪld〕*v.* 建立　　　*good news* 好消息

　　　at least 至少　　　Denmark〔ˋdɛnmark〕*n.* 丹麥

　　some…others 有些…有些　　Poland〔ˋpolənd〕*n.* 波蘭

聽力測驗（第 1-21 題，共 21 題）

第一部分：辨識句意（第 1-3 題，共 3 題）

1. (**A**) (A) (B) (C)

Joseph is reading a book when waiting for the bus.

等公車的時候，約瑟夫正在看書。

* read〔rid〕*v.* 閱讀　　***wait for*** 等待

2. (**B**) (A) (B) (C)

After the teacher entered the classroom, he saw two students fighting with each other.

老師進到教室以後，他看到兩個學生在互相打架。

* enter〔ˈɛntɚ〕*v.* 進入　　fight〔faɪt〕*v.* 打架

3. (**B**) (A) (B) (C)

The old man finds the TV program interesting, but the little girl doesn't look like she does.

老人覺得電視節目很有趣，但是小女孩看起來並不覺得如此。

* find〔faɪnd〕*v.* 覺得　　program〔'progræm〕*n.* 節目
interesting〔'ɪntrɪstɪŋ〕*adj.* 有趣的　　***look like*** 看起來像

第二部分：基本問答（第 4-10 題，共 7 題）

4.（**C**）I can't talk right now. Can I call you back?
我現在不能說話。我可以回你電話嗎？

(A) Since when? 從什麼時候？

(B) Almost there. 快到了。

(C) No problem. 沒問題。

* ***right now*** 現在　　***call sb. back*** 回某人電話

5.（**B**）How do you spell your name, Lindy?
琳蒂，妳的名字怎麼拼？

(A) I got it from my grandparents.
我從祖父母那裡得到它的。

(B) L-I-N-D-Y. L-I-N-D-Y。

(C) My name is Lindy. 我的名字是琳蒂。

* spell〔spɛl〕*v.* 拼（字）
grandparents〔'græn,pɛrənts〕*n. pl.* 祖父母

6.（**A**）Excuse me, could I use your computer?
不好意思，我可以用你的電腦嗎？

(A) Sorry. I need it right now. 抱歉。我現在要用。

(B) Thanks. You're very nice. 謝謝。你人很好。

(C) I already have one. 我已經有一台了。

* computer〔kəm'pjutɚ〕*n.* 電腦　　need〔nid〕*v.* 需要
already〔ɔl'rɛdɪ〕*adv.* 已經

7. (**A**) Hurry up! We're late. The taxi is waiting.

快點！我們遲到了。計程車在等。

(A) Give me five more minutes. 再給我五分鐘。

(B) It's not early enough. 還不夠早。

(C) The taxi driver will be late. 計程車司機會遲到。

* ***hurry up*** 趕快　　late〔let〕*adj.* 遲到的
early〔'ɝlɪ〕*adj.*（時間）早的　　driver〔'draɪvɚ〕*n.* 司機

8. (**C**) I can't believe it! I won two plane tickets from Taipei to London. 我不敢相信！我贏得兩張從台北飛倫敦的機票。

(A) I can't believe you got the job!

我不敢相信你得到那份工作。

(B) What a small world! 世界真小！

(C) You're really lucky! 你真幸運！

* believe〔bə'liv〕*v.* 相信　　win〔wɪn〕*v.* 贏得
plane ticket 機票　　London〔'lʌndən〕*n.* 倫敦
job〔dʒɑb〕*n.* 工作　　lucky〔'lʌkɪ〕*adj.* 幸運的

9. (**A**) Jack, I need to use the bathroom. You've been in there for hours. 傑克，我要上廁所。你已經在裡面幾個小時了。

(A) I'll be out in a minute. 我馬上就會出來。

(B) Sorry. Let me help you. 抱歉。讓我幫你。

(C) You don't have much time. 你沒什麼時間。

* bathroom〔'bæθ,rum〕*n.* 浴室；廁所
in a minute 立刻；馬上　　let〔lɛt〕*v.* 讓

10. (**C**) W：Can you go shopping with us on Saturday?

女：你星期六可以和我們去購物嗎？

M：I'd love to, but I have to go to school.

男：我很想去，但是我必須去學校。

(A) I'm happy to hear that. 聽到那件事我很高興。

(B) That's a good idea. 那是個好主意。

(C) That's too bad. 那真是太糟了。

* *go shopping* 去購物　*would love to* 想要
have to 必須　hear〔hɪr〕*v.* 聽到　idea〔aɪˈdiə〕*n.* 主意

第三部分：言談理解（第 11-21 題，共 11 題）

11. (**B**) W：Which one do you like? Tea, coffee or water?

女：你喜歡哪一個？茶、咖啡，或是水？

M：Water, please. My doctor doesn't want me to drink coffee and tea.

男：請給我水。我的醫生要我不要喝咖啡和茶。

Question：What does the man want? 男士要什麼？

(A) Coffee. 咖啡。

(B) Water. 水。

(C) Tea. 茶。

* coffee〔ˈkɔfɪ〕*n.* 咖啡

12. (**A**) W：Dad, I want to buy a pair of Rockets.

女：爸，我想要買一雙火箭。

M：Don't you already have three pairs of shoes?

男：妳不是已經有三雙鞋子了嗎？

W：Yes, but Rockets are different. All the sports stars wear them.

女：對，但是火箭不一樣。所有的運動明星都有穿。

Question：What are Rockets? 火箭是什麼？

(A) Shoes. 鞋子。

(B) A ball. 一顆球。

(C) A dress.　一件洋裝。

* rocket〔ˋrɑkɪt〕*n.* 火箭　　different〔ˋdɪfrənt〕*adj.* 不同的
　sport〔sport〕*n.* 運動　　star〔star〕*n.* 明星
　wear〔wɛr〕*v.* 穿

13. (**B**)　W：Oh, look at this special yellow skirt! Just three
　　　　　　thousand dollars!

　　女：噢，看看這件特別的黃色裙子！只要三千元！

　　M：It will cost you an arm and a leg. You only make ten
　　　　thousand dollars a month.

　　男：貴得要命。妳一個月只賺一萬元。

　　Question：When the man tells the woman, "It'll cost you
　　　　　　　an arm and a leg," what does he mean?

　　　　　　當男士告訴女士，「它會花掉妳一隻手臂和一條腿」，
　　　　　　他是什麼意思？

　(A) The skirt will be on sale next week.　裙子下週會特價。

　(B) The skirt is too expensive for her to buy.
　　　裙子太貴她買不起。

　(C) The skirt is too long for her.　裙子對她來說太長了。

* *cost sb. an arm and a leg*　價格昂貴；所費不貲
　on sale 廉價出售　　*too…to~*　太…以致於不~
　expensive〔ɪkˋspɛnsɪv〕*adj.* 昂貴的

14. (**B**)　W：Excuse me, sir. I bought this book yesterday and
　　　　　　found one page missing. Can I have a new one?

　　女：先生，不好意思。我昨天買了這本書，然後發現少了一頁。
　　　　我可以有一本新的嗎？

　　M：Let me see. I'm sorry, this book's been sold out. But
　　　　I can order you a new one if you don't mind waiting
　　　　for five days.

男：讓我看一下。我很抱歉，這本書已經賣完了。但是我可以幫
　　妳訂購一本新的，如果妳不介意要等五天的話。

W：Oh, that's a long time.

女：噢，那要很久。

M：Or you can choose another book at the same price.

男：或者妳可以挑選同價位的另一本書。

W：OK. I think I'll do that.

女：好。我想我會那樣做。

Question：What is the woman going to do?

　　　　　女士將會做什麼？

(A) Ask for her money back. 把她的錢要回來。

(B) Choose a different book. 挑選不同的書。

(C) Wait for the new order. 等新訂的書。

* page〔pedʒ〕*n.* 頁　　missing〔'mɪsɪŋ〕*adj.* 不見的；找不到的
  sell out 賣光　　order〔'ɔrdɚ〕*v.* 訂購　*n.* 訂貨
  mind〔maɪnd〕*v.* 介意　　choose〔tʃuz〕*v.* 選擇
  price〔praɪs〕*n.* 價格

15. (**C**) M：May I help you?

　　　　　男：我可以幫妳嗎？

W：Yes, I'd like to mail this package to Hong Kong.
　　How much should I pay?

女：可以，我想要郵寄這個包裹到香港。我應該要付多少錢？

M：Let me check. Could you write down your name and
　　phone number, please?

男：讓我看一下。請問妳能寫下妳的名字和電話號碼嗎？

W：Sure.

女：好。

M：What's inside the package?

男：包裹裡面是什麼？

W : Clothes and hats.

女：衣服和帽子。

Question : Where are the man and the woman?

男士和女士在哪裡？

(A) In a bank. 在銀行裡。

(B) In a police station. 在警察局裡。

(C) In a post office. 在郵局裡。

* mail〔mel〕*v.* 郵寄　　package〔'pækɪdʒ〕*n.* 包裹
Hong Kong〔'haŋ'kaŋ〕*n.* 香港　　pay〔pe〕*v.* 支付
check〔tʃɛk〕*v.* 查看　　sure〔ʃʊr〕*adv.* 好；當然
inside〔ɪn'saɪd〕*prep.* 在…內部　　*police station* 警察局
post office 郵局

16. (**C**) Walter's House is now open on Hope Street. When you shop at Walter's House, you can find everything you need at low, low prices. Many of the old things in the store look like new. We have beautiful clothes, special toys, useful tools, and interesting books and CDs. You won't think they were used before. Why spend lots of money buying new things? Stop by today and you will find how wonderful old things are!

瓦特的店現在在霍普街開張營業。當你在瓦特的店購物時，你可以找到每一樣你需要的東西，都是低到不行的價格。許多店裡的舊東西看起來是新的。我們有漂亮的衣服、特別的玩具、有用的工具，和有趣的書以及 CD。你不會認為它們之前被使用過。為何要花很多錢買新的東西呢？如果你今天順便過來看看，你就會發現舊的東西有多棒！

Question : What is Walter's House? 瓦特的店是什麼？

(A) A museum that collects old things.

　　一間收藏舊東西的博物館。

(B) A supermarket that sells cheaper things.

　　一間賣較為便宜的東西的超級市場。

(C) A shop that sells old things. 一間賣舊東西的店。

* house〔haʊs〕*n.* 店　　　open〔'opən〕*adj.* 開張的；營業的
　shop〔ʃɑp〕*v.* 購物　*n.* 商店　　toy〔tɔɪ〕*n.* 玩具
　tool〔tul〕*n.* 工具　　*stop by* 順道拜訪
　wonderful〔'wʌndəfəl〕*adj.* 很棒的
　museum〔mju'ziəm〕*n.* 博物館　　collect〔kə'lɛkt〕*v.* 收集
　supermarket〔'supə.mɑrkɪt〕*n.* 超級市場
　cheap〔tʃip〕*adj.* 便宜的

17. (**A**) W : Ever since the shopping center opened here, our town
　　　　　　　has not been as quiet as before. Hundreds of people
　　　　　　　and cars come in every day. The traffic is terrible.

　　女：自從購物中心開在這裡，我們的小鎮已經不像以前一樣平
　　　　靜。數以百計的人和車每天都過來。交通大亂。

　　M : Yeah, but it's easier for us to buy things, isn't it?

　　男：是的，但是我們買東西也比較容易，不是嗎？

　　W : I know the shopping center is convenient. But now
　　　　my kids often ask me to take them there to buy
　　　　things, or have some food.

　　女：我知道購物中心很方便。但是現在我的小孩常常要我帶他們
　　　　去那裡買東西，或是吃一些食物。

　　Question : What does the woman think about the
　　　　　　　shopping center? 女士認為購物中心怎麼樣？

　　(A) She doesn't really like it. 她其實不太喜歡購物中心。

　　(B) She is excited about it. 她對購物中心感到興奮。

(C) She knows nothing about it.　她對購物中心一無所知。

* ***shopping center*** 購物中心（= *mall*）
open〔'opən〕*v.* 開張；營業　　town〔taʊn〕*n.* 城鎮
quiet〔'kwaɪət〕*adj.* 平靜的；安靜的　　***hundreds of*** 數以百計的
traffic〔'træfɪk〕*n.* 交通　　terrible〔'tɛrəbḷ〕*adj.* 糟糕的
convenient〔kən'vinjənt〕*adj.* 方便的
yeah〔jɛ〕*adv.* 是的（= *yes*）　　kid〔kɪd〕*n.* 小孩
have〔hæv〕*v.* 吃　　excited〔ɪk'saɪtɪd〕*adj.* 興奮的

18. (**C**)　M：Excuse me, is this train going to Petton?

男：不好意思，這班火車要前往佩頓嗎？

W：I'm afraid we're going north.

女：恐怕我們是往北。

M：Oh no, I should go south.　I need to be in Petton by eleven.　What's the next station I need to get off?

男：噢，不，我應該要往南。我十一點前必須要到佩頓。我需要在接下來的哪一站下車？

W：We're getting close to Avon.　You can get off there.

女：我們正接近亞芬。你可以在那裡下車。

M：Thanks!

男：謝謝！

Question：What happened to the man? 男士發生什麼事？

(A) He got lost in the train station. 他在火車站迷路。

(B) He got off at the wrong station. 他下錯站。

(C) He took the wrong train. 他搭錯火車。

* ***I'm afraid***… 恐怕…　　north〔nɔrθ〕*adv.* 向北；往北
south〔saʊθ〕*adv.* 向南；往南　　by〔baɪ〕*prep.* 在…之前
next〔nɛkst〕*adj.* 下一個的；接下來的　　***get off*** 下車
close〔klos〕*adj.* 接近的　　happen〔'hæpən〕*v.* 發生
get lost 迷路　　take〔tek〕*v.* 搭乘

19. (**B**) W : Hello?

女：哈囉？

M : Hey Jenny, do you want to go see a movie today?

男：嘿，珍妮，妳今天想去看電影嗎？

W : Hmm. I don't think I can. I need to clean the house.

女：嗯。我不認為我可以。我需要打掃家裡。

M : Then can we go tomorrow?

男：那麼我們明天可以去嗎？

W : Well, I have to go to a dance class.

女：嗯，我得去上舞蹈課。

M : How about the day after tomorrow?

男：後天如何呢？

W : I'm afraid I'm going to be busy all year.

女：恐怕我一整年都會很忙。

Question : Why doesn't the woman go to see a movie
with the man? 為什麼女士不和男士去看電影？

(A) She may be too lazy. 她可能太懶惰。

(B) She may not like him. 她可能不喜歡他。

(C) She may have to stay home. 她可能必須待在家。

* clean〔klin〕*v.* 打掃   ***the day after tomorrow*** 後天
  lazy〔'lezɪ〕*adj.* 懶惰的   stay〔ste〕*v.* 待；停留

20. (**C**) Hello, this is Jenny. I just remembered the shop we're
going to won't open until twelve tomorrow. If we meet
up at eleven, we'll have to wait for an hour. Can we meet
up later? Please call me back before ten.

哈囉，我是珍妮。我剛想到明天我們要去的店十二點才會開。如
果我們十一點碰面，就必須等一個小時。我們可以晚點碰面嗎？
請在十點前回電話給我。

Question：What time may Jenny want to meet up with
　　　　　　her friend? 珍妮可能會想要幾點和她的朋友碰面？

(A) 10:00. 十點。
(B) 11:00. 十一點。
(C) 12:00. 十二點。

* ***meet up*** 碰面　　later〔ˋletɚ〕*adv.* 較晚地

21. (**A**) It's time for the top three songs on the music list this
　　　　week.　Number three is "I Still Believe".　It just came out
　　　　this Monday and has already hit number three this week.
　　　　Number two is "Listen to Your Heart".　It dropped one
　　　　place after staying on top for three weeks.　Finally,
　　　　climbing from number five, "Slow Dance" becomes our
　　　　number one!　Now, we're going to play our number one
　　　　song.

現在要來公佈本週音樂榜的前三名歌曲。第三名是「我依然相
信」。這首歌星期一才發行，本週就已經登上第三名。第二名是
「傾聽你心」。在榮登第一名三週之後，掉了一個名次。最後，
「慢舞」從第五名往上升，變成我們排行榜的第一名！現在，我
們要來播放第一名的歌曲。

Question：Which song is new on the music list this
　　　　　　week? 本週音樂榜上的新歌是哪一首？

(A) I Still Believe. 我依然相信。
(B) Listen to Your Heart. 傾聽你心。
(C) Slow Dance. 慢舞。

* ***top three*** 前三名的　　list〔lɪst〕*n.* 名單　　***come out*** 出現
hit〔hɪt〕*v.* 到達；抵達　　drop〔drɑp〕*v.* 下降
place〔ples〕*n.* 名次　　top〔tɑp〕*n.* 第一名；榜首
climb〔klaɪm〕*v.* 上升　　play〔ple〕*v.* 播放

104 年國中會考英語科試題修正意見

這份考題出得很精彩，但受到中國文化影響，難免會出一些錯誤。

題　　號	修　　正　　意　　見
第 7 題	I don't like *any one of these* three watches. → I don't like **any of these** three watches. * 應刪除 one。
第 13 題 (C)	The weather *has changed* a lot these days. → The weather **has been changing** a lot these days. * 依句意，天氣變化仍然在進行中，所以要用「現在完成進行式」，has changed 應改為 has been changing。
第 15 題 (B)	*And* don't worry if it rains. → **But** don't worry if it rains. * 依句意，語氣有轉折，應用 But。
第 20 題	When will she *possibly* go there? → When will she **probably** go there? * probably 才是美國人的習慣用法。
第 36 題 (B)	He thought what he had hoped for *became* real. → He thought what he had hoped for **had become** real. *依句意，「已經成真」，應用「過去完成式」。

104 年國中教育會考
英語科試題公佈答案

閱讀測驗

題 號	答 案	題 號	答 案
1	D	21	A
2	B	22	C
3	D	22	C
4	A	24	B
5	B	25	C
6	B	26	C
7	D	27	A
8	B	28	A
9	D	29	C
10	D	30	B
11	B	31	D
12	D	32	A
13	C	33	C
14	A	34	A
15	B	35	C
16	A	36	B
17	C	37	A
18	A	38	C
19	B	39	C
20	D	40	D

聽力測驗

題 號	答 案
1	A
2	B
3	B
4	C
5	B
6	A
7	A
8	C
9	A
10	C
11	B
12	A
13	B
14	B
15	C
16	C
17	A
18	C
19	B
20	C
21	A

103年國中教育會考英語科試題

聽力測驗（第1-20題，共20題）

第一部分：辨識句意（第1-3題，共3題）

作答說明： 第1-3題每題有三張圖片，請依據所聽到的內容，選出符合描述的圖片，每題播放兩次。

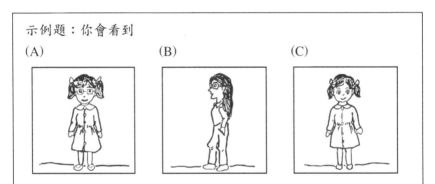

示例題：你會看到

(A)　　　　　(B)　　　　　(C)

然後你會聽到……（播音）。依據所播放的內容，正確答案應該選A，請將答案卡該題「Ⓐ」的地方塗黑、塗滿，即：● Ⓑ Ⓒ

1. (A)　　　　　(B)　　　　　(C)

2. (A)　　　　　　　(B)　　　　　　　(C)

3. (A)　　　　　　　(B)　　　　　　　(C)

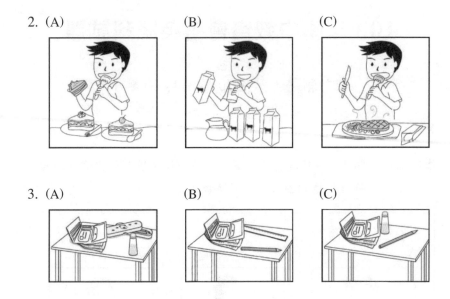

第二部分：基本問答（第 4-10 題，共 7 題）

作答說明： 第 4-10 題每題均有三個選項，請依據所聽到的內容，選出一個最適合的回應，每題播放兩次。

示例題：你會看到

(A) She is talking to the teacher.

(B) She is a student in my class.

(C) She is wearing a beautiful dress.

然後你會聽到……（播音）。依據所播放的內容，正確答案應該選 B，請將答案卡該題「Ⓑ」的地方塗黑、塗滿，即：Ⓐ ● Ⓒ

---

4. (A) I can play them well.
   (B) I don't do well at school.
   (C) I like computer.

5. (A) I'm sorry.
   (B) Sure, I'm fine.
   (C) Yes, I am a good student.

6. (A) I like to play soccer.
   (B) I went to church.
   (C) I'm going to swim.

7. (A) She's Cathy.
   (B) She's heavy.
   (C) She's twelve.

8. (A) The English class will begin in 10 minutes.
   (B) I don't know where to start.
   (C) Don't worry. You'll be OK.

9. (A) I'm sorry for you.
   (B) That's a good idea.
   (C) You did a very good job.

10. (A) He's really a good doctor.
    (B) I have to take medicine every day.
    (C) It's right in front of you.

第三部分：言談理解（第 11-20 題，共 10 題）

作答說明：第 11-20 題每題均有三個選項，請依據所聽到的內容，選出一個最適合的答案，每題播放兩次。

示例題：你會看到

(A) 9:50.　　(B) 10:00.　　(C) 10:10.

然後你會聽到……（播音）。依據所播放的內容，正確答案應該選 B，請將答案卡該題「Ⓑ」的地方塗黑、塗滿，即：Ⓐ ● Ⓒ

11. (A) To a bookstore.
    (B) To a supermarket.
    (C) To a theater.

12. (A) Go fishing.
    (B) Go to a ball game.
    (C) Have their dinner.

13. (A) Numner 543.
    (B) Number 453.
    (C) Number 345.

14. (A) A good book.
    (B) A soccer player.
    (C) A video game.

15. (A) In a gym.
    (B) In a library.
    (C) In a theater.

16. (A) It's dangerous.
    (B) It's difficult.
    (C) It's popular.

17. (A) The man should buy a
        ticket first.
    (B) The train to I-lan will
        come soon.
    (C) The train to I-lan just left.

18. (A) She'll see a movie.
    (B) She'll study for a test.
    (C) She'll take a test.

19. (A) She is a stranger to Peter.
    (B) She is Peter's friend.
    (C) She is Peter's sister.

20. (A) Dangerous animals.
    (B) Movie stars.
    (C) Sports teams.

閱讀測驗（第 21-60 題，共 40 題）

第一部分：單題（第 21-32 題，共 12 題）

21. I have to catch the bus right now, _____ I'll miss my brother's birthday party.
    (A) and
    (B) because
    (C) or
    (D) until

22. Oliver _____ with joy when he saw his favorite band. He kept saying loudly, "I love you guys!"
    (A) waited
    (B) shouted
    (C) listened
    (D) agreed

23. Ms. Lee is a(n) _____ businesswoman. Just now in her shop, she gave me back the wallet I left on the table last week.
    (A) famous
    (B) honest
    (C) important
    (D) smart

24. Lexie _____ reading maps. Even with a map, she still cannot find her way when she is in a foreign city.
    (A) is careful about
    (B) is good at
    (C) has fun
    (D) has trouble

25. More and more cows on this farm are getting sick. The problem is so _____ that the farm will be closed from tomorrow on.
    (A) heavy
    (B) popular
    (C) serious
    (D) strong

26. Some songs are forgotten very quickly. A really good song can pass the test of _____ and be remembered for many, many years.
    (A) knowledge (B) sound
    (C) time (D) weather

27. I'm not sure if Kevin _____ this morning, but if he does, I'll tell him that you called.
    (A) will come in (B) comes in
    (C) has come in (D) came in

28. I think the road ends here; it won't go any _____. Shouldn't we turn back?
    (A) closer (B) farther
    (C) faster (D) longer

29. Jogging is the only exercise I enjoy. I find _____ other kinds of exercise boring.
    (A) all (B) few
    (C) many (D) some

30. *Smart Head*, one of the hottest TV programs these days, _____ people free plane tickets to Hawaii if they can answer 20 questions correctly in 15 minutes.
    (A) have given (B) gives
    (C) giving (D) to give

31. Helen : Can you turn off the TV? I can't study with the

　　　　　_____.

　　Troy　: You can just go back to your room so you won't

　　　　　hear it.

(A) noise　　　　　　　　　(B) heat

(C) power　　　　　　　　　(D) light

32. Carson : Bye, girls. See you tomorrow, Phoebe.

　　Shirley : _____ did Carson say he would see you

　　　　　　　tomorrow?

　　Phoebe : We're going out for a picnic. Do you want to

　　　　　　　come?

(A) What　　　　　　　　　(B) When

(C) Where　　　　　　　　　(D) Why

第二部分：題組（第 33-60 題，共 28 題）

（33-35）

　　　Do you eat meat? Well, if you do, then you might
find our next news interesting. A study says that the
world has a ___33___ need for meat. In 1960, the world
ate 64 million tonnes of meat, about 21 kg for each
person. In 2007, the number rose to 268 million tonnes,
about 40 kg for each person. At the same time, ___34___.
In the 1960s, beef was high on the menu. Of the meat

that was eaten, 40% was beef. In 2007, pork became the star. Poultry also became popular, going up from 12% to 32%, thanks to people's worries about their health these years. And ___35___? You're guessing the U.S.A., right? The answer is Luxemburg! In 2007, each Luxemburger ate about 137 kg of meat! Second to Luxembourgers are Americans. In 2007, each American ate about 126 kg! Now, enough with the numbers. I'm playing you a song called *Currywurst*. The singer sings about his love for the meat dish of the same name. Enjoy!

📖 tonne 公噸   poultry 家禽（肉）

33. (A) falling　　　　　　(B) special
　　(C) growing　　　　　　(D) common

34. (A) we have changed our way of cooking meat
　　(B) new kinds of meat have come on the market
　　(C) there have been changes in the list of favorite meats
　　(D) doctors have been worried that we eat too much meat

35. (A) where does the world's best meat come from
　　(B) which country is the world's biggest meat maker
　　(C) where can you eat the world's most delicious meat
　　(D) which country uses up the most meat for each person

（36-37）

My dear friend,

　　My family and I moved into our country house one month ago. The kids are planning to give a party at our new house. I hope all of you can come. The party will begin at 11:00 a.m. on Saturday. There will be lots of food and drinks.

　　Together with this letter is a map to our house. After you get off the train, take the road in front of the station. Follow it and you'll see a chicken farm. Don't make any turns. Keep going and you'll see a bridge. Cross the bridge and there will be a big tree on your left. Walk past the tree, take the first right turn, and then walk for five more minutes. You'll see several houses. My house is at the end of the road, next to the river.

Angelica

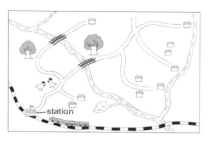

—

36. Why did Angelica invite her friends?

    (A) To see her new home.

    (B) To visit the chicken farm.

    (C) To take a train trip.

    (D) To have a picnic.

37. Look at the map. Where does Angelica live?

    (A) At Ⓐ.

    (B) At Ⓑ.

    (C) At Ⓒ.

    (D) At Ⓓ.

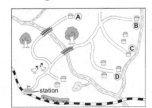

(38-39)

The Way Out

by Ming-da Wang

~~$450~~ → **$199**   <u>**Buy it now!**</u>

http://www.mingdawangbooks.net/thewayout/

Words from readers

I couldn't put the book down after I read some pages at my friend's home. I borrowed it and read it over that night. I think it can help someone who is afraid to face family problems. — Sam Lee

The book saved my life. It opened a door that led me into a world of true love. I was also able to look at the world around me with fresh new eyes. — Candy Vigor

The first part of the book really touched my heart and made me want to read on. However, I was getting bored when I came to the second part. In fact, I didn't finish the book. — Rod Green

The book helped me forget about my worries. I laughed and cried with those people in the book. With its simple and clear language, people of all ages can enjoy it. — Vivian Lu

38. Which is NOT said about the book in the reading?
    (A) It tells a true story.
    (B) It is cheaper now.
    (C) A reader thinks it is easy to understand.
    (D) A reader thinks its second part is boring.

39. What can readers most likely learn from the book?
    (A) A new way of seeing the world.　📖 likely 可能
    (B) How to be a comic writer.
    (C) A smart way to face work problems.
    (D) How to buy a book on the Internet.

（40-41）

Read the homepage of Cheetah Car Racing 2014.

Cheetah Car Racing 2014

http://www.cheetahcarracing2014.com

Still can't forget those exciting moments of Cheetah Car Racing last year in Finn City? Now it's time to get ready for this year's Cheetah Car Racing in Lynden City. Check it out now!

About Cheetah Car Racing
- The History
- 2014 Game Programs
- 2014 Race Teams

About Lynden City
- The History
- City Planning for Cheetah Car Racing 2014
- Where to Watch the Races
- Find Nice Hotels
- Eat in the City
- Shop in the City

More
- Watch the News
- Listen to the News
- Join Our Work Team
- Buy Tickets Now
- Email Us

40. Who will NOT find this homepage useful?

📖 homepage （網頁）首頁

(A) Abby, who wants to know the ticket prices.

(B) Betty, who wants to get around in Finn City.

(C) Cindy, who wants to share her ideas about car racing.

(D) Debby, who wants to collect news about the car racers.

41. Linda is reading the page of Cheetah Car Racing 2014 below.

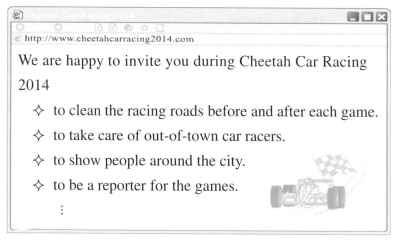

We are happy to invite you during Cheetah Car Racing 2014

◇ to clean the racing roads before and after each game.

◇ to take care of out-of-town car racers.

◇ to show people around the city.

◇ to be a reporter for the games.

⋮

Where did Linda click on the homepage of Cheetah Car Racing 2014 to get to this page?

📖 click 點擊（網頁）

(A) 2014 Game Programs.

(B) City Planning for Cheetah Car Racing 2014.

(C) Shop in the City.

(D) Join Our Work Team.

（42-44）

Cecilia： Eddie's having a tasting party this Saturday.

Gloria ： No!

Cecilia： And we're both invited.

Gloria ： No! I told you I'd never go to any of his tasting parties again!

Cecilia： He said he wanted to share his newest cakes with his dearest friends.

Gloria ： If he sees us as his dearest friends, he should stop having tasting parties!

Cecilia： Well, looks like baking really brings joy to his life.

Gloria ： But it takes joy away from mine! Last time I was in bed for three days after his party.

Cecilia： If you hate it so much, you can just tell him.

Gloria ： Why do I always have to be the bad person? Remember when I woke him up from his dream of making clothes? There was a lot of crying, and he wouldn't talk to me for a month. You do it this time.

Cecilia： I can't. How am I going to face him in our dancing classes if I tell him?

Gloria ： So we still have to lie at his party again?

Cecilia： I'm afraid so.

42. What can we learn about Eddie?

    (A) His friends think he is a great dancer.

    (B) He is taking baking classes with Cecilia.

    (C) His friends did not like the clothes he made.

    (D) He did not know how to say no to his friends.

43. Which is true?

    (A) Cecelia has not talked to Eddie for a month.

    (B) Cecelia had a good time at Eddie's last party.

    (C) Gloria shared Eddie's cakes with other friends.

    (D) Gloria does not want to go to Eddie's tasting party.

44. What does it mean?

    (A) Tell Eddie about his baking.

    (B) Tell Eddie to stop telling lies.

    (C) Tell Eddie how to find joy in baking.

    (D) Tell Eddie to stop crying over small things.

(45-47)

Below is what Josie wrote in her notebook.

Dec. 15

A very sad day. A school bus was hit by a truck. Many kids were badly hurt. A little boy lost his life. His mom was the kids' teacher. We couldn't bring her back, either.

Dec. 22

Lonnie said she'll wear all white to the Christmas party. I said she's lost her mind. We wear white all the time. Who would still want to wear white on Christmas Eve?

Dec. 25

People kept coming in and asked for our help because they got hurt. Why do people always do stupid things on holidays?

Dec. 31

The police brought in a young man who broke his leg when he was trying to enter a house. When taking care of his leg, I asked him why he wanted to enter another person's house, and he said he just wanted to borrow a pot. But Officer Clarke said he's been borrowing many pots from strangers' houses.

Jan. 3

I knew my lunchtime was over when Howell came to my table. He's a nice guy. But how many heads he's cut open is the last thing I'd want to know when I'm eating beef sandwiches.

45. Where does Josie work?

(A) In a school.   (B) In a hospital.

(C) In a restaurant.   (D) In a police station.

46. Which is true about Josie?

　(A) She did not work on Christmas because she got hurt.

　(B) She does not like what Howell talks about at lunchtime.

　(C) She lost her little boy when the school bus was hit by a truck.

　(D) She liked Lonnie's idea about what to wear for the Christmas party.

47. What do we know from the reading?

　(A) The truck driver who hit the school bus died.

　(B) Howell loves to have beef sandwiches for lunch.

　(C) Lonnie did not want to go to the Christmas party with Josie.

　(D) Officer Clarke did not think what the young man said was true.

（48-50）

G N B NEWS

Forever Takes a Bow

　　Actor Nathan Lang, 78 years old, died in his sleep last night in his house. Nathan Lang started his acting life in the 1970s. He was most known for playing Justin Maud in *Young Hours*. The movie made the world <u>swoon over</u> him.

Women wanted a husband like him; men wanted a brother like him. Forever Justin, his fans called him. After *Young Hours*, Nathan Lang was seen in several big movies; *Fallen*, *After Tonight*, and *Killing Jule*s. The last one won him a best actor award. In the 1980s, Nathan Lang lost his shine on the big screen. During this time, his movie never entered the top 20 list. Nathan Lang's last movie was *Dreams*. Though the movie won him two best actor awards, it did not bring his fans back to the theater.

This Saturday morning, 10 o'clock at St. Peter's Church, there will be a "movie party," as Lang wished. Friends and family will get together and enjoy once again the good times he brought to the world.

📖 award 獎

48. What is this reading mostly about?

   (A) Nathan Lang's love and hate for his family.

   (B) The good and bad about Nathan Lang's movies.

   (C) The rise and fall of Nathan Lang is show businesss.

   (D) Nathan Lang's life before and after he became an actor.

49. What does <u>swoon over</u> mean in the reading?

   (A) Close the door on.   (B) Go crazy about.

   (C) Share the joy with.   (D) Try hard to deal with.

50. Here are reviews about Nathan Lang's movies. From the reading, which is most likely a review for *Dreams*?

(A)

> 📖 review 評論　　likely 可能

> …nothing new in the story; Nathan Lang clearly didn't do enough homework about his part in the movie. It was no surprise that the movie didn't make it into the top 10 list the first week it was out…

(B)

> …it became Nathan Lang's second best-selling movie and also this year's third best-selling movie in the country and may even get him another best actor award…

(C)

> …see him not as the actor Nathan Lang anymore but as the poor old man in the movie. However, good acting does not always help with the ticket sales…

(D)

> …the story is fresh and interesting, but the acting is not. However, it has been the country's best-selling movie for the past three weeks. Clearly Nathan Lang's fans cared less about his acting than his handsome face…

（51-53）

Here is this year's report on the Top Ten Cities of Animal Island by *Best Living.Com.*

① **Goosetown**: Climbing up from last year's second place, Goosetown comes in first for its lovely parks, cultural centers, and comfortable living space.

② **Tigerville**: Losing its top place to Goosetown, Tigerville is still a beautiful city, and as green as ever.

③ **Duckland**: The only city staying in our top three for five years, Duckland is now cleaning itself up for next year's Football World Cup.

④ **Oxtown**: Not just a famous business city, Oxtown has turned itself into a garden city.

⑤ **Lionville**: Famous for its culture and beautiful gardens, Lionville is the first city in the north to enter our top five.

⑥ **Sharkwille**: With winter sports as good as Oxtown's, this exciting city is our second best pick in the east.

⑦ **Foxland**: This city with white beaches could rise higher in the rankings if there were fewer traffic problems.

⑧ **Goatville**: Dropping two places, Goatville should now think more about parks than shopping centers.

⑨ **Turtleland**: New in our top ten, this old fishing town is full of surprises.

⑩ **Cowtown**: Dropping from number seven, Cowtown must clean up the air.

📖 culture(-al) 文化 (的)　　ranking 排名

51. Which is NOT true about the report?
    (A) It tells us what some cities are known for.
    (B) It tells us what some cities need to deal with.
    (C) Green space plays an important part in the report.
    (D) It is the second year that *Best Living.Com* did the report.

52. What can we learn about the cities in the report?
    (A) One city in this year's top five is in the east.
    (B) Few people come to Oxtown to do business.
    (C) No city in the north entered this year's top ten.
    (D) Goosetown is Animal Island's second biggest city.

53. Which is the most likely ranking of LAST year's top ten cities of Animal Island?

📖 likely 可能

(A)

> ① Tigerville ② Goosetown ③ Cowtown ④ Oxtown
> ⑤ Duckland ⑥ Goatville ⑦ Lionville ⑧ Sharkville
> ⑨ Foxland ⑩ Turtleland

(B)

> ① Tigerville ② Goosetown ③ Duckland ④ Beartown
> ⑤ Lionville ⑥ Sharkville ⑦ Goatville ⑧ Cowtown
> ⑨ Foxland ⑩ Oxtown

(C)

> ① Goosetown ② Tigerville ③ Duckland ④ Foxland
> ⑤ Beartown ⑥ Goatville ⑦ Cowtown ⑧ Lionville
> ⑨ Oxtown ⑩ Sharkville

(D)

> ① Tigerville ② Goosetown ③ Duckland ④ Oxtown
> ⑤ Beartown ⑥ Goatville ⑦ Cowtown ⑧ Lionville
> ⑨ Foxland ⑩ Sharkville

(54-56)

> Six people are being interviewed about the garden on the roof of their building.
>
> Jasmine: I loved the idea when Wilber first told me about it. We had lost of meetings with our neighbors, trying

to make them understand why it's good to build a garden on the roof. Now people love coming here, and it's helped many of us become friends!

❖ ❖ ❖ ❖ ❖ ❖

Wilber: <u>The whole thing</u> wasn't easy at first. But Jasmine helped a lot. And she was really good at making people happy to give money for the roof garden.

❖ ❖ ❖ ❖ ❖ ❖

David: My kids love going up there. They sit there watching butterflies and birds. The roof garden brings them closer to nature.

❖ ❖ ❖ ❖ ❖ ❖

Samuel: You want something green? Visit the park! It's only block away! After the roof garden was built, bugs started flying into my apartment! And the kids leave mud on the stairs when they come down from the roof!

❖ ❖ ❖ ❖ ❖ ❖

Rosie: Our building is now cooler in the summer. My baby sleeps well even on hot summer days!

❖ ❖ ❖ ❖ ❖ ❖

Flora: Guess where these tomatoes are from! Not from the supermarket. They're from our roof! Isn't that wonderful?

📖 roof 屋頂

54. What do we know about the six people in the interview?
   (A) They all said good things about the roof garden.
   (B) Some of them were paid to help build the roof garden.
   (C) They all talked about the roof garden before it was built.
   (D) Some of them worked on the plan to build the roof garden.

55. Which of the good things about the roof garden is NOT talked about in the interview?
   (A) It brings people in the building closer together.
   (B) It uses the rainwater that falls on the top of the building.
   (C) It makes the building a more comfortable place during summer.
   (D) It gives people in the building a chance to grow their own food.

56. What does the whole thing mean in the interview?
   (A) Having meetings at the roof garden.
   (B) Taking care of the roof garden every day.
   (C) Having people agree to the idea of the roof garden.
   (D) Inviting people to make more use of the roof garden.

（57-60）

Reader's Story

It's never comfortable to take a bus during rush hour on a hot summer day. All my friends hates it. And I…, well, I ___57___ it too.

The story happened two months ago. I was on a bus that was packed with almost everyone in the city. I ___58___ my friend Neal to see a show. And then he called and said he couldn't come. "This is not what I planned for Friday!" I thought. The air on the bus was terrible; the man in front of me smelled like dead fish. While I was feeling sorry for myself, a girl called my name. I didn't recognize her at first. Then I was surprised to find that she was Hui-ting, my old neighbor. I ___59___ Hui-ting in years. We used to play together every day when we were kids. We were happy to see each other, so we decided to have dinner together. And that was the start of many dinners after.

With Hui-ting, the bus ride ___60___ something I love. The bus is still packed with people, but I enjoy the ride every day.

(Xiang Chang, Taipei)

📖 rush hour 尖峰時間　　recognize 認出

57. (A) hate   (B) have hated
     (C) used to hate   (D) would hate

58. (A) used to meet   (B) was going to meet
     (C) have met   (D) had met

59. (A) won't see   (B) wouldn't see
     (C) haven't seen   (D) hadn't seen

60. (A) has become   (B) had become
     (C) will become   (D) would become

103年國中教育會考英語科試題詳解

聽力測驗（第 1-20 題，共 20 題）

第一部分：辨識句意（第 1-3 題，共 3 題）

1. (**C**) (A)　　　　　　(B)　　　　　　(C)

Robert goes to school by bicycle. 羅伯特騎腳踏車去上學。

* **by bicycle** 騎腳踏車

2. (**C**) (A)　　　　　　(B)　　　　　　(C)

Mr. Brown likes to have steak. 伯朗先生喜歡吃牛排。

* have〔hæv〕*v.* 吃　　　steak〔stek〕*n.* 牛排

3. (**A**) (A)　　　　　　(B)　　　　　　(C)

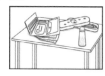

You can see a wallet, a pencil case, and glue on the desk.

你可以在書桌上看到一只皮夾、一個鉛筆盒和膠水。

* wallet〔'walɪt〕*n.* 皮夾　　　***pencil case*** 鉛筆盒

glue〔glu〕*n.* 膠水　　　desk〔dɛsk〕*n.* 書桌

第二部分：基本問答（第 4-10 題，共 7 題）

4. (**C**) Which do you like, computers or comic books?

你喜歡哪一個，電腦還是漫畫書？

(A) I can play them well. 它們我都可以彈得很好。

(B) I don't do well at school. 我在學校表現不好。

(C) I like computers. 我喜歡電腦。

* ***comic book*** 漫畫書　　***do well*** 表現好；做得好

5. (**B**) You don't look good. Are you OK?

你看起來不太好。你還好嗎？

(A) I'm sorry. 我很抱歉。

(B) Sure, I'm fine. 當然，我很好。

(C) Yes, I'm a good student. 是的，我是一位好學生。

* look〔luk〕*v.* 看起來　　sure〔ʃur〕*adv.* 的確；當然

6. (**B**) What did you do this morning? 今早你做了什麼事？

(A) I like to play soccer. 我喜歡踢足球。

(B) I went to church. 我上教堂做禮拜。

(C) I'm going to swim. 我正要去游泳。

* soccer〔'sɑkɚ〕*n.* 足球　　***go to church*** 上教堂；做禮拜

7. (**A**) Look at that girl. Do you know her?

看看那女孩。你認識她嗎？

(A) She's Cathy. 她是凱西。

(B) She's heavy. 她很重。

(C) She's twelve. 她十二歲。

* know〔no〕*v.* 知道；認識　　heavy〔'hɛvɪ〕*adj.*（重量）重的

8. (**C**) I don't think I can learn English well.
　　　　 我不認為我英文可以學得好。

　(A) The English class will begin in 10 minutes.
　　　 英文課將在十分鐘後開始。

　(B) I don't know where to start. 我不知道要從哪裡開始。

　(C) Don't worry. You'll be O.K.
　　　 別擔心。你不會有問題的。

　* learn〔lɜn〕*v.* 學習　　worry〔ˈwɜɪ〕*v.* 擔心

9. (**A**) W：Scott, what happened to your leg?
　　　　 女：史考特，你的腳怎麼了？

　　　　 M：I fell and got hurt.
　　　　 男：我跌倒受傷。

　(A) I'm sorry for you. 我真為你感到難過。

　(B) That's a good idea. 那是個好主意。

　(C) You did a very good job. 你做得很好。

　* fell〔fɛl〕*v.* 跌倒；掉落【fall 的過去式】　***get hurt*** 受傷
　happen to 發生在⋯身上　　sorry〔ˈsɔrɪ〕*adj.* 難過的
　do a good job 做得好

10. (**C**) W：Can you show me where First Hospital is?
　　　　 女：你可以告訴我第一醫院在那裡嗎？

　　　　 M：I know it's near here.
　　　　 男：我知道在這附近。

　(A) He's really a good doctor. 他真的是一位好醫生。

　(B) I have to take medicine every day. 我必須每天吃藥。

　(C) It's right in front of you. 就在你正前方。

　* show〔ʃo〕*v.* 給（人）指出（地點）　***take medicine*** 吃藥
　right〔raɪt〕*adv.* 正好；剛好　***in front of*** 在⋯的前方

第三部分：言談理解（第 11-20 題，共 10 題）

11. (**B**) W : Could you buy me some milk and bread?

女：你可以幫我買一些牛奶跟麵包嗎？

M : Right away!

男：馬上去！

Question : Where's the man going? 男士要去哪？

(A) To a bookstore. 去書局。

(B) To a supermarket. 去超級市場。

(C) To a theater. 去電影院。

* ***right away*** 馬上；立刻
bookstore〔'buk,stor〕*n.* 書局；書店
supermarket〔'supə,mɑrkɪt〕*n.* 超級市場
theater〔'θiətə〕*n.* 戲院；電影院

12. (**C**) W : I'm hungry. Can we have dinner now?

女：我好餓。我們可以現在吃晚餐嗎？

M : Sure, what would you like to have?

男：當然，妳想要吃什麼？

W : They say the seafood at that restaurant is pretty good.
What do you say?

女：他們說那家餐廳的海鮮非常棒。你覺得如何呢？

M : Good idea! Let's go!

男：好主意。我們走吧！

Question : What are they going to do?

他們即將要做什麼事？

(A) Go fishing. 去釣魚。

(B) Go to a ball game. 去看球賽。

(C) Have their dinner. 吃晚餐。

* hungry〔'hʌŋgrɪ〕*adj.* 飢餓的
  seafood〔'si,fud〕*n.* 海產食物；海鮮
  restaurant〔'rɛstərənt〕*n.* 餐廳
  pretty〔'prɪtɪ〕*adv.* 相當；非常
  What do you say? 你覺得如何？　　***ball game***　球賽

13.（ **A** ）W：Excuse me, is this bus for the train station?

女：很抱歉，這台公車有到火車站嗎？

M：No, the bus to the train station is number
five-forty-three.

男：沒有，到火車站的公車是 543 號。

W：Number…?

女：…號？

M：Five-forty-three.　Number five-forty-three.

男：543。543 號。

Question：Which bus goes to the train station?

哪台公車到火車站？

(A) Number 543.　543 號。

(B) Number 453.　453 號。

(C) Number 345.　345 號。

* ***Excuse me.*** 很抱歉。【用於引起注意力】　　***train station*** 火車站

14.（ **A** ）W：Have you ever heard about "King of the Fighter"?

女：你有聽過「戰鬥之王」嗎？

M：A…soccer player or something?

男：一位…足球選手還是什麼的嗎？

W：No, it's a great book.　I like it very much.　I'm sure
you'll like it, too.

女：不，這是一本很棒的書。我非常喜歡。我確定你也會喜歡。

Question : What's "King of the Fighter"?

什麼是「戰鬥之王」？

(A) A good book. 一本好書。

(B) A soccer player. 一位足球選手。

(C) A video game. 一個電玩遊戲。

* ***hear about*** 聽過　　fighter〔'faɪtɚ〕*n.* 戰士
player〔'pleɚ〕*n.* 選手　　sure〔ʃʊr〕*adj.* 確定的
video game 電玩遊戲

15. (**B**) M : It's almost six o'clock. How about having dinner
together?

男：快六點了。一起吃晚餐如何？

W : Thanks, but I'm not hungry yet. I'd like to study a
little longer.

女：謝謝，我還不餓。我想要再讀久一點。

Question : Where could they be? 他們可能在哪裡？

(A) In a gym. 在體育館裡。

(B) In a library. 在圖書館裡。

(C) In a theater. 在電影院裡。

* almost〔'ɔl,most〕*adv.* 幾乎；將近　　***How about …?*** …如何？
yet〔jɛt〕*adv.* 還（沒）；尚（未）　　***would like to V.*** 想要～
a little 一點；稍微　　gym〔dʒɪm〕*n.* 體育館
library〔'laɪ,brɛrɪ〕*n.* 圖書館

16. (**A**) W : I want to try roller skating.

女：我想要嘗試看看輪式溜冰。

M : You shouldn't do that. Many people get hurt when
they roller skate.

男：妳不該那麼做。很多人在輪式溜冰時受傷。

W : Then…what do you think I should do?

女： 那麼…你覺得我應該做什麼？

M : Well, maybe jogging is safer.

男： 嗯，或許慢跑比較安全。

Question : What does the man think about roller skating?

　　　　男士覺得輪式溜冰如何？

(A) It's dangerous. 很危險。

(B) It's difficult. 很困難。

(C) It's popular. 很熱門。

* ***try + V-ing*** 試看看～　　***roller skate*** *v.* 輪式溜冰

well〔wɛl〕*interj.* 嗯

maybe〔'mebɪ〕*adv.* 可能；或許

jogging〔'dʒɑgɪŋ〕*n.* 慢跑　　safe〔sef〕*adj.* 安全的

dangerous〔'dendʒərəs〕*adj.* 危險的

difficult〔'dɪfəˌkʌlt〕*adj.* 困難的

popular〔'pɑpjələ〕*adj.* 受歡迎的；熱門的

17. (**C**) M: Could I have a ticket to I-lan?

男： 我可以買一張去宜蘭的車票嗎？

W : I'm sorry, there's no train.

女： 很抱歉，沒有火車了。

M : What do you mean by "no train"?

男： 「沒有火車」是什麼意思？

W : There are no more trains to I-lan today. You just missed it.

女： 今天沒有火車去宜蘭了。你剛剛錯過了。

Question : What does the woman mean?

　　　　女士的意思是什麼？

(A) The man should buy a ticket first.

男士應該先買票。

(B) The train to I-lan will come soon.

到宜蘭的火車很快就會來。

(C) The train to I-lan just left. <u>去宜蘭的火車剛離開。</u>

* ticket〔ˈtɪkɪt〕*n.* 票；車票　　***mean ~ by…*** …的意思是 ~

just〔dʒʌst〕*adv.* 剛剛　　miss〔mɪs〕*v.* 錯過

18. (**B**) W：I can't go to see the movie with you tonight.

女：我今晚不能跟你去看電影。

M：Why not? It's a great movie!

男：為什麼不行？這是一部很棒的電影。

W：I have an important test tomorrow.

女：我明天有一個重要的考試。

Question：What will the woman do tonight?

女士今晚要做什麼？

(A) She'll see a movie. 她會去看電影。

(B) She'll study for a test. <u>她會為考試讀書。</u>

(C) She'll take a rest. 她會休息。

* ***see the movie*** 看電影　　great〔gret〕*adj.* 很棒的

take a rest 休息

19. (**B**) W：Hi Peter. I haven't seen you for a long time. How are you doing?

女：嗨，彼得。我很久沒看到你了。你還好嗎？

M：I'm fine, thank you.

男：我很好，謝謝。

W：How are your family these days?

女：你的家人近來如何？

M : They're fine, and they miss you, too. Please come see
us again when you are free.

男：他們很好，而且他們也很想念妳。妳有空的時候，請再來看
看我們。

W : I will. Bye bye.

女：我會的。再見。

Question : Who might the woman be?　女士可能是誰？

(A) She is a stranger to Peter.　她是彼得不認識的陌生人。

(B) She is a Peter's friend.　她是彼得的朋友。

(C) She is Peter's sister.　她是彼得的妹妹。

＊ ***for a long time*** 很久　　family〔ˈfæməlɪ〕*n. pl.* 家人
come see 來看看（ = *come to see* = *come and see*）
free〔fri〕*adj.* 有空的　　stranger〔ˈstrendʒɚ〕*n.* 陌生人

20. (**C**)　W : Will you go to the game with me tomorrow?

女：你明天要跟我一起去看比賽嗎？

M : You mean the Gorillas and the Bears?

男：妳是說大猩猩對上熊寶貝嗎？

W : Yes. I'm a big Bear's fan, you know. They're great.

女：是的。我是熊寶貝的超級粉絲，你知道的。他們超棒的！

M : But I think the Gorillas are better.

男：但我覺得大猩猩比較強。

Question : What are the Gorillas and the Bears?

大猩猩和熊寶貝是什麼？

(A) Dangerous animals.　危險的動物。

(B) Movie stars.　電影明星。

(C) Sports teams.　運動隊伍。

＊ gorilla〔gəˈrɪlə〕*n.* 大猩猩　　bear〔bɛr〕*n.* 熊
fan〔fæn〕*n.* 迷；粉絲

閱讀測驗（第 21-60 題，共 40 題）

第一部分：單題（第 21-32 題，共 12 題）

21. (**C**) 我現在必須去趕公車了，<u>否則</u>我會錯過我哥哥的生日派對。

    依句意，要去趕公車，「否則」會錯過派對，選 (C) *or*。
    (A) and「而且」、(B) because「因為」、(D) until「直到」，
    句意均不合。
    * catch〔kætʃ〕*v.* 趕上　　***right now***　現在

22. (**B**) 奧立佛看到他最喜歡的樂團，高興得<u>大叫</u>。他一直大聲地說：
    「我愛你們！」
    (A) wait〔wet〕*v.* 等待　　　(B) ***shout***〔ʃaut〕*v.* 大叫；喊叫
    (C) listen〔'lɪsn̩〕*v.*（注意）聽；傾聽
    (D) agree〔ə'gri〕*v.* 同意
    * joy〔dʒɔɪ〕*n.* 高興　　favorite〔'fevərɪt〕*adj.* 最喜歡的
    　band〔bænd〕*n.* 樂團　　loudly〔'laudlɪ〕*adv.* 大聲地
    　guy〔gaɪ〕*n.* 傢伙；人

23. (**B**) 李女士做生意很<u>誠實</u>。剛才在她的店裡，她把我上星期遺留在桌
    上的皮夾還給我。
    (A) famous〔'feməs〕*adj.* 有名的
    (B) ***honest***〔'ɑnɪst〕*adj.* 誠實的
    (C) important〔ɪm'pɔrtn̩t〕*adj.* 重要的
    (D) smart〔smɑrt〕*adj.* 聰明的
    * Ms.〔mɪz〕*n.* …女士
    　businesswoman〔'bɪznɪs,wumən〕*n.* 女商人
    　just now　剛剛；剛才　　leave〔liv〕*v.* 遺留

24. (**D**) 萊克西看地圖<u>有困難</u>。當她在國外的城市裡，即使有地圖，她還
    是找不到路。
    (A) be careful about　注意；小心
    (B) be good at　擅長

(C) have fun + V-ing　做某事很愉快

(D) *have trouble + V-ing*　做某事有困難

 * map〔mæp〕*n.* 地圖　　even〔'ivən〕*adv.* 即使

  way〔we〕*n.* 道路　　foreign〔'fɔrɪn〕*adj.* 外國的

25.（ **C** ）這座農場上越來越多乳牛生病了。問題非常<u>嚴重</u>，所以農場從明
天起將要關閉。

 (A) heavy〔'hɛvɪ〕*adj.* 重的；沈重的

 (B) popular〔'pɑpjələ〕*adj.* 受歡迎的

 (C) *serious*〔'sɪrɪəs〕*adj.* 嚴重的

 (D) strong〔strɔŋ〕*adj.* 強壯的

 * cow〔kaʊ〕*n.* 母牛；乳牛　　problem〔'prɑbləm〕*n.* 問題

  close〔kloz〕*v.* 關閉　　*from tomorrow on* 從明天起

26.（ **C** ）有些歌曲很快就會被遺忘。一首真正好歌可以通過<u>時間</u>的考驗，
很多很多年還會被記得。

 (A) knowledge〔'nɑlɪdʒ〕*n.* 知識

 (B) sound〔saʊnd〕*n.* 聲音　(C) *time*〔taɪm〕*n.* 時間

 (D) weather〔'wɛðə〕*n.* 天氣

 * forget〔fə'gɛt〕*v.* 忘記【三態變化為：forget-forgot-forgotten】

  quickly〔'kwɪklɪ〕*adv.* 很快地

  pass〔pæs〕*v.* 通過　　test〔tɛst〕*n.* 測驗；考驗

  remember〔rɪ'mɛmbə〕*v.* 記得

27.（ **A** ）我不確定凱文今天早上是否<u>會進來</u>，不過如果他來了，我會告訴
他你打電話來。

 if 在此作「是否」解，引導名詞子句，依句意，凱文尚未
進來，如果他進來，動作發生在未來，故應用「未來式」，
選 (A) *will come in*。因為 if 引導的是名詞子句，而不是
表「條件」的副詞子句，不須用現在現在式代替未來式，
故 (B) comes in 在此用法不合。

28.（ **B** ）我想這條路到這裡就是盡頭了；沒辦法走<u>更遠</u>。我們不應該回頭
嗎？

依句意選 (B) *farther*，是 far 的比較級，表「更遠」之意。
而 (A) closer「更近」、(C) faster「更快」、(D) longer「更長；
更久」，句意均不合。

* road〔rod〕*n.* 道路　　end〔ɛnd〕*v.* 結束；終了
go〔go〕*v.*（通路）延伸；通到　　*turn back* 返回

29. (**A**) 慢跑是我唯一喜歡的運動。我覺得所有其他種類的運動都很無趣。

依句意，除慢跑外，「所有」其他運動都很無趣，選 (A) *all*。

* jog〔dʒɑg〕*v.* 慢跑　　exercise〔'ɛksə‚saɪz〕*n.* 運動
enjoy〔ɪn'dʒɔɪ〕*v.* 喜歡　　find〔faɪnd〕*v.* 覺得
kind〔kaɪnd〕*n.* 種類　　boring〔'borɪŋ〕*adj.* 無聊的；無趣的

30. (**B**) 近來最夯的電視節目之一「金頭腦」，如果有人能在 15 分鐘
之內答對 20 個題目，要送他們免費的夏威夷機票。

主詞 *Smart Head* 為單數，one of...these days 是同位
語，空格是整句話的動詞，單數動詞應選 (B) *gives*。

* hot〔hɑt〕*adj.* 熱門的　　program〔'progræm〕*n.* 節目
these days 近來　　free〔fri〕*adj.* 免費的
plane ticket 機票　　Hawaii〔hə'waɪjə, hə'wɑjə〕*n.* 夏威夷
correctly〔kə'rɛktlɪ〕*adv.* 正確地　　minute〔'mɪnɪt〕*n.* 分鐘

31. (**A**) 海　倫：你可以把電視關掉嗎？這個噪音使我無法讀書。
特洛伊：妳只要回到你的房間，就不會聽見聲音了。

(A) *noise*〔nɔɪz〕*n.* 噪音　　(B) heat〔hit〕*n.* 熱；熱氣
(C) power〔'pauə〕*n.* 力量
(D) light〔laɪt〕*n.* 光線；亮光；燈光
* *turn off* 關掉

32. (**D**) 卡森：再見，女孩們。菲比，明天見。
雪莉：為什麼卡森說他和妳明天見？
菲比：我們要出去野餐。妳要來嗎？

由菲比的回答可知，雪莉問的是「為什麼」明天要見面，
故選 (D) *Why*。

* picnic〔'pɪknɪk〕*n.* 野餐　　*go for a picnic* 去野餐

第二部分：題組（第 33-60 題，共 28 題）

（33～35）

　　你吃肉嗎？嗯，如果你有吃的話，那你可能會覺得我們接下來的新聞很有趣。有項研究指出，全世界對於肉的需求是<u>逐漸增加的</u>。
33

在 1960 年，全世界吃了六千四百萬噸的肉，每人吃了大約 21 公斤。在 2007 年，這個數字上升到二億六千八百萬噸，每人吃了大約 40 公斤。同時，<u>最受喜愛的肉類名單已經有了改變</u>。在 1960 年代，牛肉
34

是菜單上重要的項目。在大家所吃的肉當中，有 40% 是牛肉。在 2007 年，豬肉變成了主角。家禽肉也變得受歡迎，從 12% 上升至 32%，因為人們近年來很擔心自己的健康。而<u>哪個國家平均每個人吃掉的肉最
35

多</u>？你可能會猜是美國，對吧？答案是盧森堡！在 2007 年，每個盧森堡人吃掉大約 137 公斤的肉！僅次於盧森堡人的，就是美國人。在 2007 年，每個美國人吃掉大約 126 公斤的肉！現在，數字說得夠多了。我要為大家播放一首歌，歌名是 Currywurst。這位歌手唱的是關於他對跟這首歌同名的肉類菜餚的熱愛。好好欣賞吧！

【註釋】

meat〔mit〕*n.* 肉　　then〔ðɛn〕*adv.* 那麼　　find〔faɪnd〕*v.* 覺得
next〔nɛkst〕*adj.* 接下來的　　interesting〔ˈɪntrɪstɪŋ〕*adj.* 有趣的
study〔ˈstʌdɪ〕*n.* 研究　　need〔nid〕*n.* 需求
million〔ˈmɪljən〕*n.* 百萬　　tonne〔tʌn〕*n.* 公噸（= *ton*）
kg　*n.* 公斤（= *kilogram*）　　***at the same time*** 同時
in the 1960s 在 1960 年代【即 1960-1969 年】　　beef〔bif〕*n.* 牛肉

high〔haɪ〕*adj.* 主要的；重要的；地位高的
menu〔'mɛnju〕*n.* 菜單　　of〔əv〕*prep.* 在…當中（= *among*）
pork〔pɔrk〕*n.* 豬肉　　star〔stɑr〕*n.* 明星；主角
poultry〔'poltrɪ〕*n.* 家禽（肉）【如雞、火雞、鴨、鵝等】
go up 上升　　*thanks to* 因為
worries〔'wɝɪz〕*n. pl.* 擔心；煩惱的事　　health〔hɛlθ〕*n.* 健康
these years 最近幾年　　guess〔gɛs〕*v.* 猜
Luxembourg〔'lʌksəm,bɝg〕*n.* 盧森堡【西歐國家】
Luxembourger〔'lʌksəm,bɝgɚ〕*n.* 盧森堡人　　*second to* 僅次於
American〔ə'mɛrɪkən〕*n.* 美國人　　enough〔ə'nʌf〕*pron.* 夠了
number〔'nʌmbɚ〕*n.* 數字　　play〔ple〕*v.* 為（某人）播放（唱片等）
called… 叫作…　　singer〔'sɪŋɚ〕*n.* 歌手　　dish〔dɪʃ〕*n.* 菜餚
same〔sem〕*adj.* 同樣的　　*Enjoy!* 好好欣賞吧！

33. (**C**) (A) falling〔'fɔlɪŋ〕*adj.* 減退的；降低的
　　　　 (B) special〔'spɛʃəl〕*adj.* 特別的
　　　　 (C) *growing*〔'groɪŋ〕*adj.* 增加的
　　　　 (D) common〔'kɑmən〕*adj.* 常見的；普通的

34. (**C**) (A) 我們已經改變了煮肉的方式
　　　　 (B) 好幾種新的肉已經上市
　　　　 (C) 最受喜愛的肉類名單已經有了改變
　　　　 (D) 醫生一直在擔心我們吃太多肉

　　　　 * change〔tʃendʒ〕*v. n.* 改變　　way〔we〕*n.* 方式
　　　　　 kind〔kaɪnd〕*n.* 種類　　*the market* 買賣市場；業界
　　　　　 come on the market 上市；在市場上出售（= *hit the market*）
　　　　　 list〔lɪst〕*n.* 名單　　favorite〔'fevərɪt〕*adj.* 最喜愛的

35. (**D**) (A) 全世界最好的肉來自哪裡
　　　　 (B) 哪一個國家是全世界最大的肉類製造者
　　　　 (C) 你可以在哪裡吃到全世界最好吃的肉
　　　　 (D) 哪個國家平均每個人吃掉的肉最多

　　　　 * maker〔'mekɚ〕*n.* 製造者
　　　　　 delicious〔dɪ'lɪʃəs〕*adj.* 美味的；好吃的　　*use up* 用完；吃光

（36～37）

我親愛的朋友，

　　我家人和我一個月前搬到我們鄉下的房子。小孩子們計畫要在我們的新房子舉辦派對。我希望你們都能來。派對會在週六上午十一點開始。將會有很多食物和飲料。

　　這封信附有一張來我家的地圖。在你們下火車後，走車站前面的那條路。一直走，然後你就會看到一個養雞場。不要轉彎。一直往下走，然後你們就會看到一座橋。過橋後在你的左手邊會有一棵大樹。走過那個大樹，在第一個路口右轉，然後再走五分鐘。你們會看到很多房子。我的房子就在路的盡頭，在河流旁邊。

安潔莉卡

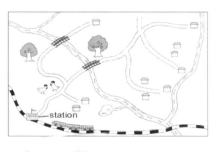

【註釋】

dear〔dɪr〕adj. 親愛的　　　move〔muv〕v. 遷移；搬家
country〔ˈkʌntrɪ〕adj. 鄉下的；鄉間的　　　plan〔plæn〕v. 打算；計畫
give a party 舉辦派對（= *have a party* = *throw a party*）
a.m. 上午；午前（= *ante meridiem*）　　　***lots of*** 很多（= *a lot of*）
food〔fud〕n. 食物　　　drink〔drɪŋk〕n. 飲料
together with 與⋯⋯一起；加上　　　***get off*** 下（車）

> **chicken farm** 養雞場 **make a turn** 轉彎 **bridge**〔brɪdʒ〕*n.* 橋
> **on** *one's* **left** 在某人的左邊 **past**〔pæst〕*prep.* 經過
> **take the right turn** 右轉 **several**〔'sɛvərəl〕*adj.* 幾個的;數個的
> **end**〔ɛnd〕*n.* 末端;盡頭 **next to** 在…旁邊

36.(**A**) 為何安潔莉卡邀請她的朋友?

    (A) 來看她的新房子。   (B) 來探訪養雞場。

    (C) 來坐火車旅行。   (D) 來野餐。

    * visit〔'vɪzɪt〕*v.* 拜訪;探訪   **take a trip** 旅行

    have a picnic 野餐

37.(**D**) 看地圖。安潔莉卡住哪裡?

    (A) 在 A。   (B) 在 B。

    (C) 在 C。   (D) 在 D。

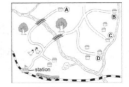

(38~39)

<<出路>>

王名大著

$450 → $199   **馬上買!**

http://www.mingdawangbooks.net/thewayout/

讀者的話

我在朋友家裡讀了幾頁後,我無法放下書本停止閱讀。我借了這本書,並在當晚讀了一遍。我覺得這本書可以幫助害怕面對家庭問題的人。——李山姆

這本書拯救了我的生命。它打開了一扇門,帶領我到真愛的世界。我能夠用新奇的眼光看我周圍的世界。——凱蒂雨果

這本書的第一個部分真的非常感動我，讓我想要繼續讀下去。然而，當我讀到第二部分，我開始感到無聊。事實上，我沒有讀完這本書。——駱德葛林

這本書幫助我忘記我的煩惱。我隨著這本書裡面的人物大笑和哭泣。這本書的語言簡單明瞭，所有年齡層的人都可以享受閱讀這本書。——盧薇薇安

【註釋】

way out 出口；出路；解決方法　　words〔wɝdz〕*n. pl.* 言語；話
put down 放下　　borrow〔'baro〕*v.* 借（入）
read over 讀一遍；從頭到尾讀完　　*be afraid to V.* 害怕～；不敢～
face〔fes〕*v.* 面對　　save〔sev〕*v.* 拯救
led〔lɛd〕*v.* 帶領；引導【lead 的過去式】　　fresh〔frɛʃ〕*adj.* 新鮮的
fresh new eyes 新奇的眼光　　touch〔tʌtʃ〕*v.* 感動
bored〔bɔrd〕*adj.* 無聊的　　*in fact* 事實上　　finish〔'fɪnɪʃ〕*v.* 結束
laugh〔læf〕*v.* 笑　　simple〔'sɪmpl̩〕*adj.* 簡單的
clear〔klɪr〕*adj.* 清楚的　　language〔'læŋgwɪdʒ〕*n.* 語言
people of all ages 所有年齡層的人　　enjoy〔ɪn'dʒɔɪ〕*v.* 享受；喜愛

38. (**A**) 關於這本書，何者「沒有」在文章裡說到？
　　　(A) <u>它敘述一個真的故事。</u>　　　(B) 它現在比較便宜。
　　　(C) 有一位讀者覺得這本書很容易了解。
　　　(D) 有一位讀者覺得它第二個部分很無聊。
　　　* reading〔'ridɪŋ〕*n.* 文選；讀物　　boring〔'borɪŋ〕*adj.* 無聊的

39. (**A**) 讀者從這本書最可能可以學到什麼？
　　　(A) <u>一種觀看世界的新方式。</u>
　　　(B) 如何成為喜劇作家。
　　　(C) 一個聰明的方式來面對工作的問題。
　　　(D) 如何在網路上買書。
　　　* likely〔'laɪklɪ〕*adv.* 可能地　　comic〔'kamɪk〕*adj.* 喜劇的
　　　writer〔'raɪtɚ〕*n.* 作者；作家　　smart〔smart〕*adj.* 聰明的
　　　on the Internet 在網路上

（40～41）

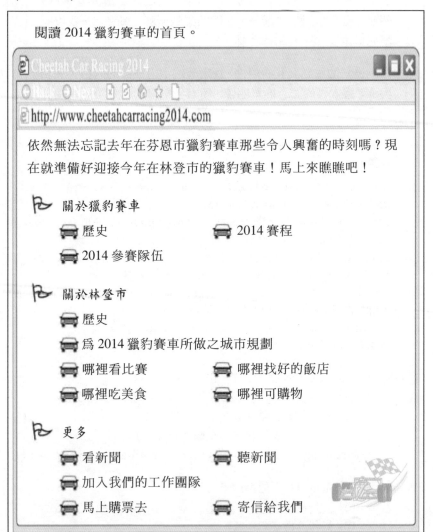

閱讀 2014 獵豹賽車的首頁。

Cheetah Car Racing 2014

Back Next

http://www.cheetahcarracing2014.com

依然無法忘記去年在芬恩市獵豹賽車那些令人興奮的時刻嗎？現在就準備好迎接今年在林登市的獵豹賽車！馬上來瞧瞧吧！

關於獵豹賽車
- 歷史
- 2014 參賽隊伍
- 2014 賽程

關於林登市
- 歷史
- 為 2014 獵豹賽車所做之城市規劃
- 哪裡看比賽
- 哪裡吃美食
- 哪裡找好的飯店
- 哪裡可購物

更多
- 看新聞
- 加入我們的工作團隊
- 馬上購票去
- 聽新聞
- 寄信給我們

【註釋】

homepage〔ˈhomˌpedʒ〕*n.*（網頁）首頁　　cheetah〔ˈtʃitə〕*n.* 獵豹
race〔res〕*v. n.* 賽跑；賽車　　still〔stɪl〕*adv.* 仍然
exciting〔ɪkˈsaɪtɪŋ〕*adj.* 令人興奮的；刺激的

moment〔'momənt〕*n.* 瞬間；片刻　　***it's time to + V.*** 該是～的時候了

get ready for *sth.* 為某事準備好　　***check out***【口語】看看；試試

history〔'hɪstərɪ〕*n.* 歷史；沿革　　game〔gem〕*n.* 比賽；活動；運動

program〔'progræm〕*n.* 程序表；節目　　team〔tim〕*n.* 隊伍

city planning 城市規劃　　hotel〔ho'tɛl〕*n.* 飯店；旅館

40. (**B**) 誰不覺得這個首頁有用？

　　(A) 艾比，想知道票價。　　(B) <u>貝蒂，想在芬恩市到處走走。</u>

　　(C) 辛蒂，想分享她對賽車的想法。

　　(D) 黛比，想收集有關賽車手的新聞。

　　* price〔praɪs〕*n.* 價錢；價格　　***get around*** 到處走動

　　　share〔ʃɛr〕*v.* 分享　　idea〔aɪ'diə〕*n.* 主意；構想

　　　collect〔kə'lɛkt〕*v.* 收集　　racer〔'resɚ〕*n.* 賽車手

41. (**D**) 琳達正在閱讀以下獵豹賽車的網頁頁面。

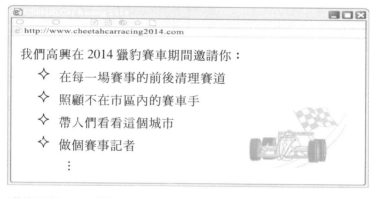

http://www.cheetahcarracing2014.com

我們高興在 2014 獵豹賽車期間邀請你：

◇ 在每一場賽事的前後清理賽道

◇ 照顧不在市區內的賽車手

◇ 帶人們看看這個城市

◇ 做個賽事記者

⋮

　　琳達點擊 2014 獵豹賽事首頁的何處到這個頁面？

　　(A) 2014 賽程。

　　(B) 為 2014 獵豹賽車所做之城市規劃。

　　(C) 哪裡可購物　　(D) <u>加入我們的工作團隊。</u>

　　* below〔bə'lo〕*adv.* 以下　　***take care of*** 照顧

　　　reporter〔rɪ'portɚ〕*n.* 記者

　　　click〔klɪk〕*v.* 點擊；發出喀嚓聲

（42～44）

賽希莉雅： 艾迪這個星期六將要舉辦一場試吃派對。

葛洛莉雅： 不！

賽希莉雅： 而且我們兩個都有被邀請。

葛洛莉雅： 不！我告訴過妳，我絕對不會再出席他的任何一場
試吃派對了。

賽希莉雅： 他說他想把最新口味的餅乾分享給最親愛的朋友。

葛洛莉雅： 如果他把我們看成是他最親愛的朋友，他應該停止
舉辦試吃派對。

賽希莉雅： 嗯，看起來烘焙真的帶給他生活樂趣。

葛洛莉雅： 但是烘焙卻帶走我生活中的歡樂！上一次參加完他
的試吃派對後，我臥床了三天。

賽希莉雅： 如果妳這麼討厭他的試吃派對，妳就告訴他。

葛洛莉雅： 為什麼我總是必須當壞人？記得我把他從想做衣服
的美夢中叫醒嗎？他哭的淅哩嘩啦的，而且一個月
不跟我說話。這次妳來跟他說。

賽希莉雅： 我不行。如果我告訴他，我要怎麼在我們的舞蹈課
面對他？

葛洛莉雅： 所以我們還是要在他的試吃派對上說謊囉？

賽希莉雅： 恐怕是如此。

【註釋】

taste〔test〕*v.* 品嘗；試吃　　party〔ˈpartɪ〕*n.* 派對；宴會
have a party 舉辦一場派對　　both〔boθ〕*n.* 兩者；雙方

invite〔ɪn'vaɪt〕*v.* 邀請　　　***stop + V-ing*** 停止
baking〔'bekɪŋ〕*n.* 烘焙；烘烤　　***take away*** 帶走；拿走
mine〔maɪn〕*n.* 我的～【I 的所有代名詞】　　***last time*** 上一次
in bed 在床上　　***be the bad person*** 當壞人
wake sb. up 把某人叫醒　　dream〔drim〕*n.* 夢想；願望
a lot of 許多　　***have to*** 必須　　lie〔laɪ〕*v.* 撒謊
afraid〔ə'fred〕*adj.* 害怕的；恐怕

42.(**C**) 關於艾迪，我們可以得知什麼？

　　(A) 他的朋友認為他是一位優秀的舞者。

　　(B) 他跟賽希莉雅一起上烘焙課。

　　(C) 他的朋友不喜歡他做的衣服。

　　(D) 他不知道如何向他的朋友說不。

　　* dancer〔'dænsɚ〕*n.* 舞者　　***take classes*** 上課
　　　say no 拒絕

43.(**D**) 何者為真？

　　(A) 賽希莉雅已經一個月沒跟艾迪說話了。

　　(B) 賽希莉雅在艾迪上次的派對玩得很開心。

　　(C) 葛洛莉雅分享艾迪的餅乾給其他的朋友。

　　(D) 葛洛莉雅不想去艾迪的試吃派對。

　　* ***have a good time*** 過得很愉快；玩得很痛快

44.(**A**) it 是什麼意思？

　　(A) 告訴艾迪關於他的烘焙。

　　(B) 告訴艾迪不要再說謊了。

　　(C) 告訴艾迪如何從烘焙中找到樂趣。

　　(D) 告訴艾迪停止為了小事而哭泣。

　　* ***tell lies*** 說謊話

（45～47）

以下爲裘西在她的筆記本寫下的內容。

12 月 15 日
非常悲傷的一天。有台校車被一輛卡車撞到。很多孩童嚴重受傷。一個小男孩失去他的生命。他的媽媽是這群孩童的老師。我們也無法救回他。

12 月 22 日
蘿妮說她將會穿一身白去聖誕舞會。我說她瘋了。我們一直以來都穿白的。誰還會想在聖誕夜穿白色？

12 月 25 日
人們持續地進來，並且請求我們幫忙，因爲他們受傷了。爲什麼人們總是在假日期間做蠢事？

12 月 31 日
警方帶來一位年輕人，他試圖進入一戶民宅時弄斷了自己的腿。當在照料他的腿的時候，我問他爲什麼想進去別人的房子，他說他只是想借個鍋子。但是克拉克警官說，這位年輕人一直從陌生人的房子裡借了很多鍋子。

1 月 3 日
當豪威爾來到我的桌旁時，我知道我的午餐時間結束了。他是個好人。但當我吃著牛肉三明治時，我最不想知道的，就是他開過多少人的頭。

【註釋】

notebook〔ˈnotˌbʊk〕*n.* 筆記本　　sad〔sæd〕*adj.* 悲傷的

school bus 校車　　hit〔hɪt〕*v.* 撞到　　truck〔trʌk〕*n.* 卡車
badly〔'bædlɪ〕*adv.* 嚴重地　　hurt〔hɜt〕*v.* 傷害
lose one's life 失去生命　　*not… either* 也不…
lose one's mind 發瘋；失去理智　　*all the time* 一直
eve〔iv〕*n.* 前夕　　keep〔kip〕*v.* 持續　　*ask for* 要求
stupid〔'stjupɪd〕*adj.* 愚蠢的　　*on holidays* 在假日
the police 警方　　break〔brek〕*v.* 折斷　　enter〔'ɛntɚ〕*v.* 進入
take care of 照顧　　borrow〔'baro〕*v.* 借（入）
pot〔pat〕*v.* 鍋；罐；壺　　officer〔'ɔfəsɚ〕*n.* 警官
stranger〔'strendʒɚ〕*n.* 陌生人　　lunchtime〔'lʌntʃ,taɪm〕*n.* 午餐時間
cut open 切開　　*the last* 最不…的　　beef〔bif〕*n.* 牛肉
sandwich〔'sændwɪtʃ〕*n.* 三明治

45. (**B**) 裘西在哪裡工作？

　　(A) 在學校。　　　　　　(B) 在醫院。
　　(C) 在餐廳。　　　　　　(D) 在警察局。
　　* hospital〔'haspɪtl〕*n.* 醫院　　restaurant〔'rɛstərənt〕*n.* 餐廳
　　　police station 警察局

46. (**B**) 關於裘西，下列何者為真？

　　(A) 她在聖誕節不用工作，因為她受傷了。
　　(B) 她不喜歡豪威爾在午餐時間說的話。
　　(C) 在校車被卡車撞到時，她失去了她的兒子。
　　(D) 她喜歡蘿妮要穿什麼去聖誕舞會的想法。
　　* *talk about* 談論　　idea〔aɪ'diə〕*n.* 想法

47. (**D**) 從本文我們可以得知什麼？

　　(A) 那個撞到校車的卡車司機死了。
　　(B) 豪威爾喜歡午餐吃牛肉三明治。
　　(C) 蘿妮不想跟裘西一起去聖誕舞會。
　　(D) 克拉克警官不認為那個年輕人說的話是真的。
　　* reading〔'ridɪŋ〕*n.* 文章　　true〔tru〕*adj.* 真的

（48～50）

GNB 新聞

永遠的謝幕

　　演員內桑雷恩，昨晚於睡夢中在自己家中過世，享年78歲。內桑雷恩，在1970年代開始他的演藝人生。他最知名的是在電影「年輕時光」中飾演賈斯汀莫德。這部電影讓全世界都為他神魂顛倒。女人都想要像他一樣的丈夫；而男人想要像他一樣的兄弟。他的影迷們都稱他為永遠的賈斯汀。繼「年輕時光」之後，他也演了許多強檔大片：「墮落」、「今晚過後」、「追殺茱勒」。而「追殺茱勒」讓他獲得最佳男演員獎。在1980年代，內桑雷恩失去了大銀幕上的光芒。在這段期間，他的電影從沒進過排行榜的前20名。內桑雷恩的最後一部電影是「夢」，雖然這部電影讓他獲得兩次最佳男演員獎，但是卻沒有讓他的影迷再次回到電影院裡。

　　這禮拜六早上十點，在聖彼得教堂，將會如雷恩所願，舉辦一場「電影饗宴」。朋友和家人將會聚集在一起，再次享受他帶給世界的那些好時光。

【註釋】

* forever〔fə'ɛvɚ〕adv. 永遠　　bow〔baʊ〕n. 鞠躬
take a bow 鞠躬謝幕　　sleep〔slip〕n. 睡覺
start〔stɑrt〕v. 開始　　acting〔'æktɪŋ〕adj. 演戲的
in the 1970s 在 1970 年代　　most〔most〕adv. 最
known〔non〕adj. 知名的　　play〔ple〕v. 扮演
swoon〔swun〕v. 陶醉；著迷　　***swoon over*** 對～神魂顛倒
husband〔'həzbənd〕n. 丈夫　　fan〔fæn〕n. 迷

call〔kɔl〕v. 稱呼　　several〔'sɛvərəl〕adj. 數個的

big〔bɪg〕adj. 偉大的；重要的

won〔wʌn〕v. 使（某人）贏得【win 的過去式】

actor〔'æktə〕n. 演員　　award〔ə'wɔrd〕n. 獎

lost〔lɔst〕v. 失去【lose 的過去式】　　shine〔ʃaɪn〕n. 光芒

screen〔skrin〕n. 螢幕；（電影的）銀幕

during〔'durɪŋ〕prep. 在…期間　　never〔'nɛvə〕adv. 從未

enter〔'ɛntə〕v. 進入　　**top 20** 前 20 名　　list〔lɪst〕n. 名單

though〔ðo〕conj. 雖然　　**bring sb. back to** 使某人回到

theater〔'θiətə〕n. 電影院　　church〔tʃɝtʃ〕n. 教堂

wish〔wɪʃ〕v. 希望　　**get together** 聚集

enjoy〔ɪn'dʒɔɪ〕v. 享受　　**once again** 再一次

times〔taɪmz〕n. pl. 時光　　bring〔brɪŋ〕v. 帶

world〔wɝld〕n. 世界

48. (**C**) 本文主要是關於什麼？

(A) 內桑雷恩對家人的愛與恨。

(B) 內桑雷恩電影的優點和缺點。

(C) 內桑雷恩在演藝事業的起起落落。

(D) 內桑雷恩在成為演員之前和之後的人生。

* reading〔'ridɪŋ〕n. 文章　　mostly〔'mostlɪ〕adv. 主要地

rise〔raɪz〕n. 上升　　fall〔fɔl〕n. 下降

rise and fall 起起落落；興衰　　show〔ʃo〕n. 表演

business〔'bɪznɪs〕n. 事業　　**show business** 演藝事業

49. (**B**) swoon over 在本文中是什麼意思？

(A) 把門關上。　　　　(B) 為之瘋狂。

(C) 分享喜悅。　　　　(D) 努力試著處理。

* **close the door on** sb. 對某人關門　　go〔go〕v. 變得

crazy〔'krezɪ〕adj. 瘋狂的；迷戀的　　share〔ʃɛr〕v. 分享

joy〔dʒɔɪ〕n. 喜悅　　**deal with** 應付；處理

50. (**C**) 以下是關於內桑雷恩的影評。從這篇文章中，哪個選項最有可能是「夢」的評論？

(A)

> …故事了無新意；內桑雷恩很顯然沒有為他在電影裡面的角色做足功課。電影沒有在剛上映的時候進入排行榜前十名，一點都不令人驚訝…

(B)

> …這變成內桑雷恩第二暢銷的電影，也是今年全國第三暢銷的電影，很有可能讓他獲得另一座最佳演員獎…

(C)

> …看看他在這部電影裡面一點都不像演員內桑雷恩，而是像一個可憐的老先生。然而，精湛的演技不一定對票房有幫助…

(D)

> …這部電影新鮮有趣，但是演技卻不是。然而，這是全國過去三週以來最賣座的電影。顯然相較於演技，內桑雷恩的影迷們比較在意的是他英俊的外表…

* nothing 〔ˈnʌθɪŋ〕*pron.* 沒有
clearly 〔ˈklɪrlɪ〕*adv.* 清楚地　　enough 〔əˈnʌf〕*adj.* 足夠的
homework 〔ˈhomˌwɜk〕*n.* 功課　　part 〔part〕*n.* 角色
surprise 〔səˈspraɪz〕*v. n.* 驚訝　　***make it*** 成功
out 〔aut〕*adv.* 出現；問世　　best-selling *adj.* 最暢銷的
also 〔ˈɔlso〕*adv.* 也　　get 〔gɛt〕*v.* 使獲得
country 〔ˈkʌntrɪ〕*n.* 國家　　another 〔əˈnʌðɚ〕*adj.* 另一個的
not…anymore 不再…　　however 〔hauˈɛvɚ〕*adv.* 然而
not always 未必；不一定　　past 〔pæst〕*adj.* 過去的
less 〔lɛs〕*adv.* 較不　　handsome 〔ˈhænsəm〕*adj.* 英俊的

（51～53）

以下是今年由「最佳生活網」關於對動物島嶼的前 10 名城市的報導。

① **鵝　　市**：從去年的第二名攀升到第一名，鵝市因為它可愛的公園、文化中心，和舒適的生活空間而拔得頭籌。

② **老虎市**：第一名的位置輸給了鵝市，老虎市還是很美麗的城市，一如往常的綠草如茵。

③ **小鴨市**：唯一連續五年位居前三名的城市，小鴨市現在為了明年的世足賽而清理環境。

④ **公牛市**：不僅是一個很有名的商業城市，公牛市已經轉變成花園城市。

⑤ **獅子市**：以文化和美麗的花園聞名，獅子市是第一個進入前 5 名的北方城市。

⑥ **鯊魚市**：和公牛市有一樣優異的冬季運動，這個令人興奮的城市是我們東部挑選出來第二好的。

⑦ **狐狸市**：這個城市有白色的沙灘會增進排名，如果交通問題少一點的話，排名應該會更高。

⑧ **山羊市**：跌落兩名，山羊市現在應該思考公園而不是購物中心。

⑨ **烏龜市**：第一次進入前十名，這個古老的漁業城鎮充滿了驚喜。

⑩ **乳牛市**：從第七名下滑，乳牛市必須清理空氣。

【註釋】

report〔rɪˋport〕*n.* 報告　　animal〔ˋænəml̩〕*n.* 動物
island〔ˋaɪlənd〕*n.* 島嶼　　goose〔gus〕*n.* 鵝　　***climb up*** 攀升

second place 第二名　　*come in first* 得第一名

lovely〔ˋlʌvlɪ〕*adj.* 可愛的　　cultural〔ˋkʌltʃərəl〕*adj.* 文化的

center〔ˋsɛntɚ〕*n.* 中心　　comfortable〔ˋkʌmfɚtəbḷ〕*adj.* 舒適的

living〔ˋlɪvɪŋ〕*adj.* 生活的　　space〔spes〕*n.* 空間

tiger〔ˋtaɪgɚ〕*n.* 老虎　　lose〔luz〕*v.* 失去　　*top place* 第一名

green〔grin〕*adj.* 綠色的；環保的　　*as…as ever* 跟以前一樣…

duck〔dʌk〕*n.* 鴨子　　stay〔ste〕*v.* 停留　　*clean up* 清理

Football World Cup 世界盃足球賽　　ox〔ɑks〕*n.* 公牛

famous〔ˋfeməs〕*adj.* 有名的　　*turn…into~* 使…轉變成~

garden〔ˋgɑrdṇ〕*n.* 花園　　lion〔ˋlaɪən〕*n.* 獅子

north〔nɔrθ〕*n.* 北方　　enter〔ˋɛntɚ〕*v.* 進入

shark〔ʃɑrk〕*n.* 鯊魚　　sport〔sport〕*n.* 運動

exciting〔ɪkˋsaɪtɪŋ〕*adj.* 令人興奮的　　pick〔pɪk〕*n.* 所挑選之物

east〔ist〕*n.* 東方　　fox〔fɑks〕*n.* 狐狸　　beach〔bitʃ〕*n.* 海灘

ranking〔ˋræŋkɪn〕*n.* 排名；等級　　traffic〔ˋtræfɪk〕*n.* 交通

drop〔drɑp〕*v.* 下降　　goat〔got〕*n.* 山羊

shopping center 購物中心　　turtle〔ˋtɝtḷ〕*n.* 烏龜

fishing〔ˋfɪʃɪŋ〕*n.* 漁業　　*be full of* 充滿了　　cow〔kaʊ〕*n.* 母牛

51.（**D**）關於這篇報導哪一項不是真的？

　　　(A) 它告訴我們一些城市為什麼有名。

　　　(B) 它告訴我們一些城市有什麼是需要處理的。

　　　(C) 綠地在報導中扮演很重要的角色。

　　　(D) 這是最佳生活網第二年做這個報導。

　　　* *be known for* 因…而有名　　*deal with* 應付；處理

　　　 play an important part 扮演重要的角色

52.（**A**）關於這些城市，我們可以從這篇報導中得知什麼?

　　　(A) 今年前五名中的一個城市是在東部。

　　　(B) 很少人去公牛市做生意。

　　　(C) 北方沒有城市進入今年的前十名。

　　　(D) 鵝市是動物島嶼中的第二大城市。

　　　* learn〔lɝn〕*v.* 得知　　*do business* 做生意

53.(**D**) 哪一個最有可能是去年動物島嶼的前十名排名?

(A)

①老虎市	②鵝　市	③乳牛市	④公牛市	⑤小鴨市
⑥山羊市	⑦獅子市	⑧鯊魚市	⑨狐狸市	⑩烏龜市

(B)

①老虎市	②鵝　市	③小鴨市	④大熊市	⑤獅子市
⑥鯊魚市	⑦山羊市	⑧乳牛市	⑨狐狸市	⑩公牛市

(C)

①鵝　市	②老虎市	③小鴨市	④狐狸市	⑤大熊市
⑥山羊市	⑦乳牛市	⑧獅子市	⑨公牛市	⑩鯊魚市

(D)

①老虎市	②鵝　市	③小鴨市	④公牛市	⑤大熊市
⑥山羊市	⑦乳牛市	⑧獅子市	⑨狐狸市	⑩鯊魚市

(54～56)

六個人正接受採訪，談論關於他們大樓屋頂的花園。

茉　莉：當威爾伯最初告訴我關於這件事的時候，我喜愛這個點子。我們和鄰居開了很多會，試圖讓他們了解為什麼在屋頂上蓋花園很好。現在人們喜愛來這，而且幫助我們許多人成為朋友！

◆　◆　◆　◆　◆　◆

威爾伯：這整件事起初並不容易。但是茉莉幫了大忙。而且她真的很擅長讓人們樂於為了屋頂花園付錢。

◆　◆　◆　◆　◆　◆

大　衛：我的孩子們喜愛上去那裡。他們坐在那裡觀賞蝴蝶和鳥。屋頂花園使他們更親近大自然。

◆　◆　◆　◆　◆　◆

山　謬：你想要綠油油的事物？去造訪公園！它只有一個街區之遠！在屋頂花園蓋好後，蟲子開始飛進我的公寓！而當孩童們從屋頂上下來時，他們會在樓梯上留下泥巴！

◆　◆　◆　◆　◆　◆

蘿　西：現在我們的大樓在夏天的時候比較涼爽。我的寶寶甚至在炎熱的夏日也能睡得好！

◆◆◆◆◆◆

芙蘿拉：猜猜這些蕃茄是從哪來的！不是超級市場。它們是從我們的屋頂來的！那不是很棒嗎？

【註釋】

interview〔ˈɪntɚˌvju〕v. n. 訪談；面談　　roof〔ruf〕n. 屋頂
building〔ˈbɪldɪŋ〕n. 建築物；大樓　　meeting〔ˈmitɪŋ〕n. 會議
neighbor〔ˈnebɚ〕n. 鄰居　　try〔traɪ〕v. 試圖
understand〔ˌʌndɚˈstænd〕v. 了解　　build〔bɪld〕v. 建造
become〔bɪˈkʌm〕v. 成為　　whole〔hol〕adj. 全部的；整個的
be good at 善於；擅長　　give〔gɪv〕v. 付出　　kid〔kɪd〕n. 小孩
butterfly〔ˈbʌtɚˌflaɪ〕n. 蝴蝶　　bring〔brɪŋ〕v. 使
close〔klos〕adj. 親近的　　nature〔ˈnetʃɚ〕n. 大自然
green〔grin〕adj. 綠油油的　　block〔blɑk〕n. 街區
apartment〔əˈpɑrtmənt〕n 公寓　　leave〔liv〕v. 留下
mud〔mʌd〕n. 泥巴　　stairs〔stɛrs〕n. pl. 樓梯
cool〔kul〕adj. 涼爽的　　guess〔gɛs〕v. 猜
tomato〔təˈmeto〕n. 蕃茄　　wonderful〔ˈwʌndɚˌfəl〕adj. 很棒的

54. (**D**) 關於在訪談中的六個人，我們知道什麼？

(A) 他們全部都說屋頂花園的好事。

(B) 他們當中有些人有領薪水來幫忙蓋屋頂花園。

(C) 在屋頂花園蓋好以前，他們都在談論它。

(D) 他們當中有些人致力於蓋屋頂花園的計畫。

＊pay〔pe〕v. 支付（薪水）　　***work on*** 致力於

55. (**B**) 關於屋頂花園的好事，哪一項沒有在訪談中被談到？

(A) 它使大樓內的人們彼此更為緊密。

(B) 它利用落在樓頂上的雨水。

(C) 它使大樓在夏天成為一個更舒適的地方。

(D) 它給大樓內的人們一個機會來種植他們自己的食物。

```
* together〔tə`gɛðə〕adv. 一起；相互地　　use〔juz〕v. 利用
  rainwater〔`ren,wɔtə〕n. 雨水　　fall〔fɔl〕v. 降落
  chance〔tʃæns〕n. 機會　　grow〔gro〕v. 種植
```

56. (**C**) 訪談裡的 <u>the whole thing</u> 是什麼意思？

　　(A) 在屋頂花園開會。　　　　(B) 每天照顧屋頂花園。

　　(C) 讓人們同意屋頂花園的點子。

　　(D) 邀請人們多加利用屋頂花園。

　　* mean〔min〕v. 意思是　　***make use of*** 利用

（57～60）

讀者的故事

　　在炎炎夏日的尖峰時間搭公車絕對不舒適。我所有的朋友都討厭這件事。而我…，嗯，我<u>以前</u>也<u>討厭</u>這件事。
　　　　　　　　　　　　　　57　　57

　　故事是發生在兩個月前。我在一輛幾乎擠進市內所有人的公車上。<u>我正要和</u>我的朋友尼爾<u>碰面</u>去看表演。
　　　　　　　　　　58　　　　　　　58

接著他打電話給我，說他不能來。「這不是我計畫的星期五！」我心裡想。公車上的空氣很糟；在我前方的男士聞起來像死魚。當我正在為自己感到難過的時候，有個女生叫了我的名字。我起初沒有認出她。然後我很驚訝地發現她是我的老鄰居，惠婷。我<u>有</u>很多年<u>不見</u>惠婷了。我們以
　　　　　　　　　　　　　　　　59

前小時候每天都一起玩。我們見到彼此很高興，所以我們決定一起吃晚餐。而且那次也是之後許多次晚餐的開端。

　　因為惠婷，搭公車已<u>變成</u>我喜愛的事物。公車還是擠
　　　　　　　　　　　　60

滿了人，但是我每天都很享受搭車。

（張翔，台北）

【註釋】

reader〔ˈridɚ〕*n.* 讀者　　story〔ˈstorɪ〕*n.* 故事

rush〔rʌʃ〕*adj.* 匆促的　　***rush hour*** （交通）尖峰時刻

hate〔het〕*v.* 討厭　　happen〔ˈhæpən〕*v.* 發生

month〔mʌnθ〕*n.* 月　　pack〔pæk〕*v.* 使擠進

almost〔ˈɔlˌmost〕*adv.* 幾乎　　city〔ˈsɪtɪ〕*n.* 城市

show〔ʃo〕*n.* 表演　　call〔kɔl〕*v.* 打電話；叫

plan〔plæn〕*v.* 計劃　　air〔ɛr〕*n.* 空氣

terrible〔ˈtɛrəbḷ〕*adj.* 可怕的　　***in front of*** 在…前面

smell〔smɛl〕*v.* 聞起來　　sorry〔ˈsɔrɪ〕*adj.* 難過的

recognize〔ˈrɛkəgˌnaɪz〕*v.* 認出

surprised〔səˈpraɪzd〕*adj.* 驚訝的

find〔faɪnd〕*v.* 發現　　***in years*** 好幾年　　***used to*** 以前

decide〔dɪˈsaɪd〕*v.* 決定　　have〔hæv〕*v.* 吃

start〔stɑrt〕*n.* 開始　　ride〔raɪd〕*n.* 乘坐；搭乘

enjoy〔ɪnˈdʒɔɪ〕*v.* 享受；喜歡

57.（**C**） 依句意，選 (C) ***used to hate***「以前討厭」。

58.（**B**） 依句意，選 (B) ***was going to meet***「正要去和…見面」。

59.（**D**） 過去某一時間已完成的動作，須用「過去完成式」，又，

張翔是過去一段時間沒有見到惠婷，故選 (D) ***hadn't seen***。

60.（**A**） 從過去持續到現在的動作，須用「現在完成式」，又，

張翔從見到惠婷後，到現在搭車「已變成」他喜愛的事情，

故選 (A) ***has become***。

103 年國中教育會考英語科試題修正意見

※ 這份考題出得很精彩，但受到中國文化影響，容易出現一些錯誤。

題　　號	修　　正　　意　　見
第 35 題 (D)	which country *uses up* the most meat *for each* person → which country **eats** the most meat **per** person * 根據句意，「哪個國家平均每個人吃掉的肉最多」，所以 uses up 應改為 eats 或 consumes，for each person 應改為 per person。
第 40 題 (D)	Debby, who wants to *collect* news about the car racers. → Debby, who wants to **read** news about the car racers. * 美國人習慣「讀」新聞，而不是「收集」新聞，所以 collect 應改為 read。
第 48-50 題 倒數第 3 行	This Saturday morning, 10 o'clock at St. Peter's Church, ... → This Saturday morning, *at* 10 o'clock at St. Peter's Church, ... * 表示幾點鐘，須用介系詞 at。This Saturday morning 是名詞片語當副詞用【詳見「文法寶典」p.100】可改成 On Saturday morning，但是 10 o'clock 前需要介系詞 at。
第 50 題 第 1 行	Here are reviews *about* Nathan Lang's movies. → Here are reviews *of* Nathan Lang's movies. * 表「…的評論」，用 reviews of 或 comments about。
第 50 題 (B)(D)	*best-selling* → ***most popular*** 或 ***most successful*** * best-selling（暢銷的）是指商品的銷售，例如 DVD，不可用於電影，所以應改為 most popular（最受歡迎的）或 most successful（最成功的）。

103 年度國中教育會考
英語科公佈答案

題 號	答 案	題 號	答 案	題 號	答 案
1	C	21	C	41	D
2	C	22	B	42	C
3	A	23	B	43	D
4	C	24	D	44	A
5	B	25	C	45	B
6	B	26	C	46	B
7	A	27	A	47	D
8	C	28	B	48	C
9	A	29	A	49	B
10	C	30	B	50	C
11	B	31	A	51	D
12	C	32	D	52	A
13	A	33	C	53	D
14	A	34	C	54	D
15	B	35	D	55	B
16	A	36	A	56	C
17	C	37	D	57	C
18	B	38	A	58	B
19	B	39	A	59	D
20	C	40	B	60	A

電腦統計歷屆國中會考英文單字

a.m. （103 會考）

able （103~105 會考）

about （103~105 會考）

above （105 會考）

acting （103、105 會考）

actor （103、104 會考）

adjacent （105 會考）

afraid （103~105 會考）

after （103、104 會考）

afternoon （105 會考）

again （103~105 會考）

age （103~105 會考）

ago （103、105 會考）

agree （103~105 會考）

ahead （105 會考）

air （103 會考）

airplane （105 會考）

all （103~105 會考）

almost （103~105 會考）

alrcady （104、105 會考）

also （103~105 會考）

always （103~105 會考）

American （103、105 會考）

animal （103~105 會考）

another （103~105 會考）

answer （103、104 會考）

any （104、105 會考）

anymore （103 會考）

anyone （105 會考）

anything （104、105 會考）

apartment （103、104 會考）

appear （104、105 會考）

applause （105 會考）

April （104 會考）

area （105 會考）

arm （104、105 會考）

around （103~105 會考）

arrive （104 會考）

art （104、105 會考）

as （103~105 會考）

ask （103~105 會考）

asleep （104、105 會考）

attack （105 會考）

aunt （104 會考）

average （104 會考）

award （103 會考）

away （103~105 會考）

baby （103~105 會考）

back （103~105 會考）

bad （103~105 會考）

badly （103 會考）

bake （105 會考）

baker （105 會考）

bakery （104、105 會考）

baking （103、105 會考）

balcony （105 會考）

ball （103~105 會考）

banana （104 會考）

band （103 會考）

bank （104 會考）

bar （104 會考）

baseball （105 會考）

basketball （105 會考）

bath （104 會考）

bathroom （104 會考）

beach （103、105 會考）

bear （103 會考）

beautiful （103~105 會考）

because （103~105 會考）

become （103~105 會考）

bed （103 會考）

beef （103 會考）

before （103~105 會考）

begin （103~105 會考）

believe （104、105 會考）

belong （104 會考）

below （103~105 會考）

best （103~105 會考）

best-selling （103 會考）

better （104 會考）

between （104、105 會考）

bicycle （103 會考）

big （103~105 會考）

bird （103、105 會考）

birthday （103~105 會考）

bite （105 會考）

black （105 會考）

blind （104 會考）

block （103 會考）

blow （105 會考）

blue （104 會考）

boat （105 會考）

book （103～105 會考）

bookstore （103、104 會考）

bored （103 會考）

boring （103、105 會考）

borrow （103、105 會考）

boss （105 會考）

both （103 會考）

bowl （105 會考）

boy （103～105 會考）

bread （103、105 會考）

break （103、105 會考）

bridge （103 會考）

bright （105 會考）

bring （103～105 會考）

brother （103～105 會考）

brush （105 會考）

bug （103 會考）

build （103、104 會考）

building （103、104 會考）

burn （105 會考）

burning （104 會考）

bus （103～105 會考）

business （103～105 會考）

businesswoman

（103 會考）

busy （104 會考）

but （103～105 會考）

butter （105 會考）

butterfly （103、105 會考）

buy （103～105 會考）

buyer （104 會考）

buzz （105 會考）

cake （103、104 會考）

calamitous （104 會考）

call （103～105 會考）

candy （104、105 會考）

car （104、105 會考）

card （104、105 會考）

care （103～105 會考）

careful （103 會考）

carry （104 會考）

case （103、105 會考）

cat （105 會考）

catch （103、105 會考）

caught （105 會考）

CD （104 會考）

cell phone （104、105 會考）

center （103、104 會考）

chance （103、104 會考）

change （103～105 會考）

chart （104、105 會考）

cheap （103、104 會考）

check （103、104 會考）

cheese （104、105 會考）

chicken （103～105 會考）

child （105 會考）

children （104、105 會考）

chocolate （104 會考）

choose （104 會考）

Christmas （103 會考）

church （103、104 會考）

church-goer （104 會考）

circle （104 會考）

city （103、105 會考）

class （103～105 會考）

classmate （105 會考）

classroom （104 會考）

clean （103、104、105 會考）

clear （103、105 會考）

clearly （103 會考）

click （103 會考）

climb （103、104 會考）

close （103～105 會考）

closed （105 會考）

clothes （103、104 會考）

cocoon （105 會考）

coffee （104、105 會考）

cola （104 會考）

cold （104、105 會考）

collect （103、104 會考）

color （104、105 會考）

comb （105 會考）

come （103～105 會考）

comfortable （103、104 會考）

comic （103 會考）

comics （105 會考）

coming （104 會考）

common （103 會考）

computer （103～105 會考）

convenient （104 會考）

cook （103～105 會考）

cooking （104 會考）

cool （103、104 會考）

correctly （103 會考）

cost （104 會考）

cough （105 會考）

could （103、104 會考）

country （103～105 會考）

couple （105 會考）

course （104、105 會考）

cover （105 會考）

cow （103、105 會考）

crazy （105 會考）

cross （103、105 會考）

crowd （105 會考）

cry （103、105 會考）

cultural （103 會考）

culture （103 會考）

cup （103 會考）

cut （103 會考）

dad （104 會考）

dance （104 會考）

dancer （103 會考）

dancing （103、105 會考）

dangerous （103、105 會考）

dark （104、105 會考）

date （104、105 會考）

daughter （105 會考）

day （103~105 會考）

dead （103~105 會考）

deal （103~105 會考）

dear （103~105 會考）

decide （103~105 會考）

delicious （103、104 會考）

department （104 會考）

desk （103 會考）

dialogue （105 會考）

die （103~105 會考）

different （104、105 會考）

differently （105 會考）

difficult （103、104 會考）

dinner （103、105 會考）

dirty （104 會考）

dish （103 會考）

do （103~105 會考）

doctor （103~105 會考）

dog （105 會考）

dollar （104、105 會考）

door （103~105 會考）

Do-Re-Me （105 會考）

dot （104 會考）

down （103~105 會考））

draw （104、105 會考）

dream （103~105 會考）

dreamer （105 會考）

dreamland （104 會考）

dress （103~105 會考）

drink （103~105 會考）

driver （103~105 會考）

drop （103~105 會考）

dry （105 會考）

during （103~105 會考）

dying （104、105 會考）

each （103~105 會考）

early （104 會考）

earth （104 會考）

east （103、105 會考）

easy （103~105 會考）

eat （103~105 會考）

egg （105 會考）

either （103~105 會考）

else （105 會考）

Email （103 會考）

e-mail （104 會考）

end （103~105 會考）

England （105 會考）

English （103、105 會考）

enjoy （103~105 會考）

enough （103~105 會考）

enter （103、104 會考）

eve （103 會考）

even （103~105 會考）

evening （105 會考）

ever （103、104 會考）

every （103~105 會考）

everyday （104 會考）

everyone （103~105 會考）

everything （104、105 會考）

everywhere （105 會考）

example （104、105 會考）

excellent （105 會考）

except （104、105 會考）

excited （104、105 會考）

exciting （103~105 會考）

excuse （103~105 會考）

exercise （103 會考）

exoplanet （104 會考）

expensive （104 會考）

experience （104、105 會考）

experiment （104 會考）

eye （104、105 會考）

face （103、105 會考）

fact （103、104 會考）

fall （103~105 會考）

fallen （103 會考）

family （103~105 會考）

famous （103、104 會考）

fan （103、105 會考）

far （104 會考）

farm （103~105 會考）

farther （103 會考）

fast （103~105 會考）

father （104 會考）

favorite （103~105 會考）

feel （103~105 會考）

festival （105 會考）

few （103~105 會考）

fight （104 會考）

fighter （103 會考）

figure （104 會考）

finally （104、105 會考）

find （103~105 會考）

findings （104 會考）

fine （103、105 會考）

finish （103~105 會考）

fire （105 會考）

first （103~105 會考）

fish （103、105 會考）

fishing （103 會考）

flower （104、105 會考）

fly （103~105 會考）

follow （103~105 會考）

food （103~105 會考）

football （103 會考）

foreign （103 會考）

forever （103 會考）

forget （103~105 會考）

free （103 會考）

freely （104 會考）

fresh （103 會考）

Friday （103、104 會考）

friend （103~105 會考）

frog （104 會考）

front （103 會考）

fruit （104 會考）

full （103、104 會考）

fun （103 會考）

funny （104 會考）

future （104 會考）

game （103~105 會考）

garbage （105 會考）

garden （103、104 會考）

gas （104 會考）

gate （104、105 會考）

get （103~105 會考）

ghost （105 會考）

giant （104 會考）

gift （104、105 會考）

girl （103~105 會考）

girlfriend （105 會考）

give （103~105 會考）

glass （104、105 會考）

glue （103 會考）

go （103~105 會考）

golden （104 會考）

good （103~105 會考）

gorilla （103 會考）

grade （105 會考）

grandparents （104 會考）

grape （104 會考）

gray （105 會考）

great （103~105 會考）

green （103 會考）

ground （105 會考）

grow （103、104 會考）

guess （103、104 會考）

guy （103、105 會考）

gym （103~105 會考）

habit （104 會考）

hair （105 會考）

half （104 會考）

Halloween （105 會考）

hand （105 會考）

handsome （103、105 會考）

happen （103、104 會考）

happy （103~105 會考）

hard （103~105 會考）

hat （104 會考）

hate （103、104 會考）

have （103~105 會考）

Hawaii （103 會考）

head （103、105 會考）

health （103、105 會考）

hear （103、104 會考）

heart （103、104 會考）

heat （103、104 會考）

heavily （104 會考）

heavy （103、105 會考）

hello （104、105 會考）

help （103～105 會考）

her （105 會考）

here （103～105 會考）

herself （105 會考）

hey （104、105 會考）

hi （103、105 會考）

hide （105 會考）

high （103～105 會考）

hill （104 會考）

himself （105 會考）

history （103、105 會考）

hit （103～105 會考）

hmm （104、105 會考）

hobby （104、105 會考）

holiday （103 會考）

home （104、105 會考）

homepage （103 會考）

homework （103、105 會考）

honest （103～105 會考）

Hong Kong （104 會考）

hop （104 會考）

hope （103～105 會考）

horse （104 會考）

hospital （103～105 會考）

hot （103、104 會考）

hotel （103 會考）

hour （103～105 會考）

hours （104 會考）

house （103～105 會考）

housework （105 會考）

how （103～105 會考）

however （103～105 會考）

hundred （104 會考）

hungry （103 會考）

hunt （104 會考）

hurry （104 會考）

hurt （103、105 會考）

husband （103、105 會考）

ice （104 會考）

idea （103～105 會考）

if （103～105 會考）

important （103～105 會考）

inside （104、105 會考）

interest （104 會考）

interested （104、105 會考）

interesting （103～105 會考）

Internet （103、104 會考）

interview （103～105 會考）

into （103 會考）

invite （103、105 會考）

island （103、105 會考）

Italian （105 會考）

itself （103、104 會考）

job （103～105 會考）

jog （103 會考）

join （103～105 會考）

joy （103～105 會考）

juice （104 會考）

July （105 會考）

jump （104 會考）

June （105 會考）

just （103～105 會考）

keep （103～105 會考）

key （105 會考）

kg （103 會考）

kick （105 會考）

kid （103、104 會考）

kill （104 會考）

killer （105 會考）

killing （103 會考）

kind （103、105 會考）

king （103～105 會考）

kitchen （104 105 會考）

knock （104 會考）

know （103～105 會考）

knowledge （103、104 會考）

known （103、104 會考）

language （103 會考）

large （104 會考）

last （103～105 會考）

late （104 會考）

later （104、105 會考）

laugh （103、105 會考）

lazy （104 會考）

lead （103、104 會考）

leader （105 會考）

learn （103～105 會考）

least （104、105 會考）

leave （103 會考）

left （103～105 會考）

leg （103～105 會考）

less （103～105 會考）

lesson （104 會考）

let （104 會考）

let's （103、105 會考）

letter （103 會考）

library （103、105 會考）

lie （103 會考）

life （103～105 會考）

light （103、104 會考）

like （103～105 會考）

likely （103～105 會考）

line （104、105 會考）

lion （104 會考）

list （103～105 會考）

listen （103～105 會考）

little （103～105 會考）

live （104、105 會考）

living （103、105 會考）

London （104 會考）

lonely （105 會考）

long （103～105 會考）

look （103～105 會考）

lose （103～105 會考）

lost （104、105 會考）

lot （103、104 會考）

lots （103、104 會考）

loudly （103 會考）

lousy （104 會考）

love （103～105 會考）

lovely （103、105 會考）

low （104 會考）

luck （104 會考）

luckily （105 會考）

lucky （104、105 會考）

lunch （103～105 會考）

lunchtime （103 會考）

mad （105 會考）

magic （104 會考）

mail （104、105 會考）

make （103～105 會考）

maker （103 會考）

man （103～105 會考）

many （103～105 會考）

move （103～105 會考）

movie （103～105 會考）

moving （105 會考）

Mr. （105 會考）

Ms. （103～105 會考）

much （103～105 會考）

mud （103、105 會考）

museum （104、105 會考）

music （104、105 會考）

must （103、105 會考）

must （會考）

myself （103～105 會考）

name （103～105 會考）

national （104 會考）

nature （103 會考）

near （103～105 會考）

need （103～105 會考）

neighbor （103、104 會考）

never （103～105 會考）

new （103～105 會考）

news （103～105 會考）

next （103～105 會考）

nice （103～105 會考）

night （103、105 會考）

nightclub （104 會考）

noise （103 會考）

noodles （105 會考）

noon （104 會考）

nope （105 會考）

north （103～105 會考）

notebook （103 會考）

nothing （103～105 會考）

notice （105 會考）

now （103～105 會考）

number （103～105 會考）

o'clock （103 會考）

off （104 會考）

office （104、105 會考）

officer （103、105 會考）

often （104、105 會考）

oh （104、105 會考）

OK （103～105 會考）

old （103～105 會考）

once （103、104 會考）

online （104 會考）

only （103～105 會考）

open （103～105 會考）

or （104、105 會考）

orange （104 會考）

order （104、105 會考）

other （103～105 會考）

others （104 會考）
our （103～105 會考）
out （103～105 會考）
out-of-town （103 會考）
outside （104 會考）
over （103～105 會考）
own （103～105 會考）

p.m. （104、105 會考）
package （104 會考）
packed （103 會考）
page （103、104 會考）
paint （105 會考）
painting （105 會考）
pair （104 會考）
paper （105 會考）
parent （105 會考）
parents （104、105 會考）
park （103、105 會考）
part （103～105 會考）
party （103、104 會考）
pass （103、105 會考）
past （103～105 會考）.
pay （103～105 會考）
PE （105 會考）
pencil （103 會考）
people （103～105 會考）
percentage （104、105 會考）
perhaps （104 會考）
person （103、104 會考）
pet （104、105 會考）
phone （104、105 會考）
photo （105 會考）

piano （105 會考）
pick （103～105 會考）
picnic （103 會考）
picture （104、105 會考）
pie （104 會考）
pinky （105 會考）
place （103～105 會考）
plan （103～105 會考）
plane （103、104 會考）
planet （104 會考）
play （103～105 會考）
player （103、104 會考）
playground （105 會考）
please （103～105 會考）
pleasure （105 會考）
pm （104 會考）
poem （105 會考）
point （104 會考）
police （103～105 會考）
police station （104 會考）
polite （104、105 會考）
pond （104 會考）
poor （103、104 會考）
popular （103、105 會考）
pork （103 會考）
possible （104、105 會考）
possibly （104、105 會考）
post （104、105 會考）
post office （104 會考）
poster （104 會考）
pot （103、104 會考）
poultry （103 會考）
pound （104 會考）
power （103～105 會考）
pray （104 會考）

preface （104 會考）
prepare （104 會考）
pretty （103、104 會考）
price （103、104 會考）
prize （105 會考）
problem （103～105 會考）
program （104、105 會考）
proud （105 會考）
pull （105 會考）
pumpkin （104 會考）
puppy （105 會考）
purple （105 會考）
put （104 會考）

question （103～105 會考）
quickly （103 會考）
quiet （104 會考）

race （103、105 會考）
racer （103 會考）
racing （103 會考）
radio （105 會考）
rain （104 會考）
rainwater （103 會考）
ranking （103 會考）
read （103～105 會考）
reader （103 會考）
reading （103～105 會考）
ready （103、105 會考）
real （104、105 會考）

really （103～105 會考）
recognize （103 會考）
refrigerator （105 會考）
remember （103～105 會考）
report （103～105 會考）
reporter （103 會考）
rest （103、104 會考）
restaurant （103～105 會考）
restroom （105 會考）
review （103 會考）
ride （103、105 會考）
rider （105 會考）
right （103 會考）
right （104 會考）
right （105 會考）
ring （104、105 會考）
rise （103、105 會考）
rising （104 會考）
road （103、105 會考）
rocket （104 會考）
roller skate （103 會考）
roof （103 會考）
room （103、105 會考）
round （105 會考）
rule （104、105 會考）
run （105 會考）
runner （105 會考）
rush （103 會考）

sad （103、104 會考）
safe （103、105 會考）
sail （105 會考）
salad （105 會考）

sale （104、105 會考）
sales （103、105 會考）
same （103～105 會考）
same-sex （105 會考）
sandwich （103、104 會考）
Saturday （103～105 會考）
save （103～105 會考）
say （103～105 會考）
scared （105 會考）
schedule （105 會考）
school （103～105 會考）
science （105 會考）
screen （103、105 會考）
sea （105 會考）
seafood （103～105 會考）
season （105 會考）
second （103、105 會考）
see （103～105 會考）
sell （104、105 會考）
sentence （104 會考）
serious （103～105 會考）
seriously （105 會考）
several （103、105 會考）
sex （105 會考）
shake （104、105 會考）
shape （105 會考）
share （103、104 會考）
sharply （104 會考）
shine （103、104 會考）
shoes （104、105 會考）
shop （103～105 會考）
shopkeeper （105 會考）
shopping （103～105 會考）
short （104 會考）
should （103～105 會考）
shoulder （104 會考）

shout （103 會考）
show （103～105 會考）
sick （103～105 會考）
sidewalk （105 會考）
simple （103 會考）
simply （104 會考）
since （104、105 會考）
sing （103、105 會考）
singer （103 會考）
sir （104 會考）
sister （103～105 會考）
sit （103、105 會考）
size （105 會考）
skirt （104 會考）
sleep （103、105 會考）
slow （104、105 會考）
slowly （104 會考）
slump （105 會考）
small （103～105 會考）
smell （105 會考）
smile （104、105 會考）
snake （104 會考）
so （103～105 會考）
soccer （103 會考）
solar （104 會考）
soldier （105 會考）
some （103～105 會考）
someone （104、105 會考）
something （103～105 會考）
somewhere （105 會考）
song （103104 會考）
soon （103～105 會考）
sorry （103、104 會考）
sound （103～105 會考）
south （104、105 會考）

space （103、104 會考）

speaker （105 會考）

special （103～105 會考）

spell （104 會考）

spend （104、105 會考）

sport （104 會考）

sports （103～105 會考）

spring （105 會考）

square （104 會考）

stair （103 會考）

stand （105 會考）

star （103、104 會考）

start （103～105 會考）

state （104、105 會考）

station （103～105 會考）

stay （103～105 會考）

steak （103、105 會考）

still （103～105 會考）

stop （103～105 會考）

store （104、105 會考）

story （103～105 會考）

storybook （104 會考）

straight （104 會考）

stranger （103、105 會考）

street （104、105 會考）

strong （103～105 會考）

student （103～105 會考）

study （103～105 會考）

stupid （103 會考）

subject （104 會考）

summer （103～105 會考）

sun （105 會考）

sunny （104 會考）

supermarket （103～105 會考）

super-smart （104 會考）

sure （103～105 會考）

surprise （103～105 會考）

surprised （103、104 會考）

surprising （105 會考）

swear （103 會考）

sweet （105 會考）

swim （103～105 會考）

swimming （104、105 會考）

system （104 會考）

table （103、104 會考）

Taipei （104 會考）

take （103～105 會考）

talk （103～105 會考）

tall （104 會考）

taste （103、105 會考）

taxi （104、105 會考）

tea （104 會考）

teach （104 會考）

teacher （103～105 會考）

team （103～105 會考）

tell （103、104、105 會考）

tennis （104、105 會考）

terrible （103、104 會考）

test （103 會考）

than （103～105 會考）

thank （103～105 會考）

thanks （103～105 會考）

that （103、104、105 會考）

theater （103～105 會考）

their （103～105 會考）

them （103 會考）

themselves （104 會考）

then （103～105 會考）

there （103～105 會考）

these （103、104 會考）

they （103、104 會考）

thin （104 會考）

thing （103～105 會考）

think （103～105 會考）

thinking （105 會考）

third （103、105 會考）

this （103～105 會考）

those （104、105 會考）

though （103～105 會考）

thousand （104 會考）

throat （105 會考）

Thursday （104、105 會考）

ticket （103、104 會考）

time （103～105 會考）

times （103～105 會考）

tired （104、105 會考）

tiring （105 會考）

today （103～105 會考）

to-do list （104 會考）

together （103～105 會考）

tomato （103、105 會考）

tomorrow （103、104 會考）

tonight （103～105 會考）

too （103～105 會考）

tool （104 會考）

top （104 會考）

total （104 會考）

totally （104、105 會考）

touch （103、105 會考）

town （103～105 會考）

toy （104、105 會考）

traffic （103、104 會考）

train （103～105 會考）

trash （105 會考）

tree （103 會考）

trip （104 會考）

trouble （103、104 會考）

truck （103 會考）

true （103、105 會考）

try （103～105 會考）

Tuesday （105 會考）

turn （103～105 會考）

TV （103～105 會考）

twice （104 會考）

U.S.A. （103 會考）

umm （105 會考）

uncle （104 會考）

under （104、105 會考）

understand （103 會考）

until （103、104 會考）

up （103～105 會考）

use （103～105 會考）

used （103～105 會考）

useful （103、104 會考）

vacation （104、105 會考）

very （103～105 會考）

video （103 會考）

visit （103～105 會考）

voice （104、105 會考）

wait （103～105 會考）

waiter （104、105 會考）

waitress （105 會考）

wake （103、104 會考）

walk （104、105 會考）

wall （104、105 會考）

wallet （103、105 會考）

want （103、105 會考）

warm （104、105 會考）

watch （103～105 會考）

watchdog （104 會考）

water （104、105 會考）

way （103～105 會考）

weak （104 會考）

wear （103～105 會考）

weather （103～105 會考）

Wednesday （104、105 會考）

week （103～105 會考）

weekend （104 會考）

welcome （104、105 會考）

well （103～105 會考）

well-paid （104 會考）

wet （104 會考）

whale （105 會考）

what （103～105 會考）

when （103～105 會考）

where （103～105 會考）

whether （105 會考）

which （103～105 會考）

while （103、104 會考）

whisper （105 會考）

white （103、105 會考）

who （103～105 會考））

whole （103 會考）

why （103～105 會考）

wife （104、105 會考）

win （103～105 會考）

wind （105 會考）

window （105 會考）

winter （103 會考）

wish （103、105 會考）

without （104、105 會考）

woman （103～105 會考）

wonderful （103～105 會考）

word （103～105 會考）

work （105 會考）

world （103～105 會考）

worry （103～105 會考）

worse （104 會考）

worst （105 會考）

would （103～105 會考）

wow （105 會考）

write （103～105 會考）

writer （103、104 會考）

wrong （104、105 會考）

yeah （104、105 會考）

year （103～105 會考）

yellow （104 會考）

yesterday （104、105 會考）

yet （103～105 會考）

you （103～105 會考）

young （103～105 會考）

your （103～105 會考）

電腦統計歷屆國中會考英文成語

a few （105 會考）

a lot （103、104 會考）

a lot of （103 會考）

a pair of （104 會考）

a second （104 會考）

after school （105 會考）

agree to N. （103 會考）

agree with （104、105 會考）

all the time （103 會考）

all year round （105 會考）

almost there （104 會考）

answer *one's* call （104 會考）

anyone who （105 會考）

arrive at （104 會考）

as before （104 會考）

as fast as his legs can carry him （104 會考）

as...as （103～105 會考）

as…as ever （103 會考）

as…as one can （104 會考）

ask for （104、105 會考）

ask for *one's* help （103 會考）

ask for *one's* money back （104 會考）

ask *sb.* to V. （105 會考）

at any time （105 會考）

at first （103 會考）

at least （104、105 會考）

at lunchtime （103 會考）

at noon （104 會考）

at one time （105 會考）

at school （103、105 會考）

at that moment （104 會考）

at the end of （103 會考）

at the first turn （104 會考）

at the same price （104 會考）

at the same time （103、105 會考）

away from home （105 會考）

be able to V. （103~105 會考）

be adjacent to （105 會考）

be afraid of （104、105 會考）

be badly hurt （103 會考）

be blind to （104 會考）

be burning hot （104 會考）

be careful about （103 會考）

be covered with （105 會考）

be excited about （104 會考）

be famous for （103、104 會考）

be full of （103、104 會考）

be going to V. （103~105 會考）

be good at （103、104 會考）

be interested in （104、105 會考）

be known as （104 會考）

be known for （103 會考）

be lousy at （104 會考）

be made of （104 會考）

be married to （104 會考）

be nothing like （104 會考）

be packed with （103 會考）

be proud of （105 會考）

be put to other uses （104 會考）

be scared of （105 會考）

be sure to V. （105 會考）

be tired of （104 會考）

be true with （105 會考）

because of （104、105 會考）

become crazy （105 會考）

become real （104 會考）

begin *one's* turn （104 會考）

believe in （105 會考）

belong to （104 會考）

between *A* and *B* （105 會考）

break *one's* leg （103 會考）

bring *sb.* closer to nature （103 會考）

burn down （105 會考）

by bicycle （103 會考）

by boat （105 會考）

by e-mail （104 會考）

by oneself （105 會考）

call sb. back （104 會考）

can't wait to V. （104 會考）

care about （103、105 會考）

care for （105 會考）

catch cold （105 會考）

catch the bus （103 會考）

center around （104 會考）

change *A* into *B* （105 會考）

change from *A* to *B* （105 會考）

cheaper things （104 會考）

Check it out （103 會考）

clean itself up （103 會考）

clean out （105 會考）

clean up the air （103 會考）

clear throat （105 會考）

climb up （103 會考）

close the door on

（103 會考）

come down （103 會考）

come in （103、104 會考）

come on the market

（103 會考）

come out （104 會考）

come to an end （105 會考）

comes in first （103 會考）

cost *sb.* an arm and a leg

（104 會考）

cry over *sth.* （103 會考）

deal with （103~105 會考）

decide to V. （103、104 會考）

die from （104 會考）

do a good job （103 會考）

do business （103~105 會考）

do the housework

（105 會考）

do the report （103 會考）

do well （103 會考）

down there （105 會考）

drop sharply （104 會考）

during this time （103 會考）

each other （104、105 會考）

end up V-ing （104 會考）

enjoy + V-ing （104、105

會考）

enough to V. （104 會考）

enough with （103 會考）

even if （104 會考）

even so （104 會考）

ever since （104 會考）

every day （103、104 會考）

every time （105 會考）

every week （105 會考）

except for （104 會考）

excuse me （103、104 會考）

fall asleep （104、105 會考）

fall on *one's* shoulders

（104 會考）

fewer and fewer （104 會考）

find out （104、105 會考）

for a long time （103、104

會考）

for days （105 會考）

for example （104 會考）

for hours （104 會考）

for long （104 會考）

for nothing （105 會考）

for years （104 會考）

forget about （105 會考）

forget to V. （104 會考）

from the start （105 會考）

from tomorrow on

（103 會考）

get around （103 會考）

get close to （104 會考）

get hurt （103、105 會考）

get lost （104 會考）

get married （105 會考）

get off （103、104 會考）

get ready （105 會考）

get *sth.* back （105 會考）

get to （103~105 會考）

get to V. （104 會考）

get up （104 會考）

get worse （104 會考）

getg wet （104 會考）

give a party （103 會考）

give back （103 會考）

give up （104、105 會考）

go ahead （105 會考）

go away （105 會考）

go back to （103、104 會考）

go crazy about （103 會考）

go fishing （103 會考）

go out for a picnic

（103 會考）

go out with *sb.* （105 會考）

go see a movie （104 會考）

go shopping （104 會考）

go the wrong way

（105 會考）

go to （105 會考）

go to a class （104 會考）

go to church （103、104

會考）

go to school （103~105 會考）

go to see a movie （103、

104 會考）

go to the game （103 會考）

go up （103 會考）

go well （105 會考）

good and bad （104 會考）

Good idea! （103 會考）

Good job. （105 會考）

grow up （104 會考）

happen to （103、104 會考）

happy and sad （104 會考）

hard work （104 會考）

have a bath （104 會考）

have a date with *sb.*

（105 會考）

have a dream （105 會考）

have a good time （103、104 會考）

have a long way to go （104 會考）

have a meeting （103 會考）

have a party （103 會考）

have a pet （104 會考）

have a picnic （103 會考）

have a test （103 會考）

have a wonderful tim （105 會考）

have dinner （103 會考）

have food （104 會考）

have fun （103 會考）

have lunch （104 會考）

have no problem + V-ing （105 會考）

have no voice in （104 會考）

have steak （103 會考）

have *sth.* all to oneself （104 會考）

have to V （103、104 會考）

heard about （103 會考）

help with （103 會考）

Here we are. （105 會考）

hit number three （104 會考）

hop into （104 會考）

hope for （104 會考）

How about...? （103～105 會考）

How are you doing? （103 會考）

how long （104 會考）

How much...? （104、105 會考）

hundreds of （104 會考）

hurry out of （104 會考）

Hurry up! （104 會考）

I can't wait. （105 會考）

I'm afraid （104 會考）

I'm afraid so （103 會考）

in a minute （104 會考）

in class （104 會考）

in fact （103 會考）

in front of （103 會考）

in *one's* everyday life （104 會考）

in *one's* mind （104 會考）

in the afternoon （105 會考）

in the east （103 會考）

in the end （104 會考）

in the future （104 會考）

in the north （105 會考）

in the south （105 會考）

in town （104 會考）

It is no surprise that （103 會考）

it is time for *sb.* to V. （104 會考）

It's time for... （104 會考）

it's time to V. （103 會考）

just like （104 會考）

keep + V-ing （103～105 會考）

keep *sb.* from （104 會考）

knock down （104 會考）

know more about （104 會考）

know nothing about （104 會考）

last time （103、105 會考）

lead to （104 會考）

learn about （103～105 會考）

leave a message （104 會考）

less and less （104 會考）

less than （105 會考）

Let's go! （103 會考）

Let's see （105 會考）

like + V-ing （104 會考）

listen to （103、104 會考）

live it to the fullest （104 會考）

look around （104 會考）

look at （103～ 會考）

look for （104、105 會考）

look like （103～105 會考）

lose *one's* mind （103 會考）

lose sth. to *sb.* （103 會考）

lose to （105 會考）

lost interest in （104 會考）

lost *sb.* to sth. （104 會考）

lots of （103、104 會考）

love + V-ing （103、105 會考）

make a mistake （105 會考）

make a plan （105 會考）

make a turn （103 會考）

make friends （104 會考）

make it （103 會考）

many times （104 會考）

meet up with *sb.* （104、105 會考）

mind + V-ing （104 會考）

more and more （103 會考）

more than （104、105 會考）

move away （105 會考）

move into （103 會考）

move up north （105 會考）

my thanks go to （105 會考）

need to V. （105 會考）

next to （103、104 會考）

next week （104 會考）

no idea （105 會考）

No problem. （104、105 會考）

not always （103 會考）

Not at all. （105 會考）

not yet （104 會考）

not...at all （105 會考）

not...until （104 會考）

not…anymore （103 會考）

not…either （103 會考）

not…yet （103 會考）

of all ages （103、105 會考）

of course （104 會考）

on a date （105 會考）

on Christmas （103 會考）

on Christmas Eve （103 會考）

on fire （105 會考）

on holidays （103 會考）

on paper （105 會考）

on sale （104 會考）

on Saturday （104 會考）

on the desk （103 會考）

on the Internet （103、104 會考）

on the street （105 會考）

once again （103 會考）

one day （104 會考）

one last time （105 會考）

open *one's* arms to （105 會考）

or something （103 會考）

out there （105 會考）

over a low heat （104 會考）

over the years （105 會考）

over time （104 會考）

pass by （105 會考）

pass the test of time （103 會考）

pay for （104、105 會考）

pick up （104、105 會考）

plan to V. （103、105 會考）

play a part （104 會考）

play an important part （103、104 會考）

play basketball （105 會考）

play computer games （104 會考）

play *sb.* a song （103 會考）

play soccer （103 會考）

play sports （104 會考）

pull *sb.* down （105 會考）

put down （103 會考）

rain heavily （104 會考）

rain or shine （104 會考）

read on （103 會考）

read over （103 會考）

remember to V. （104 會考）

right away （103 會考）

right now （103、104 會考）

run after （105 會考）

run away （105 會考）

rush hour （103 會考）

sail out （105 會考）

say good things about （103 會考）

say no to *sb.* （103 會考）

second place （103 會考）

second to （103 會考）

see *A* as *B* （103、105 會考）

see a movie （103 會考）

share *sth.* with *sb.* （104 會考）

show *sb.* around （105 會考）

show *sb.* around the city （103 會考）

so…that （103、104 會考）

sold out （104 會考）

some…others （104 會考）

sound like （104 會考）

spend money (in) + V-ing （104 會考）

spend *one's* vacation （105 會考）

spend time + V-ing （104 會考）

spend two hours + V-ing （105 會考）

start + V-ing （103、105 會考）

start a family （105 會考）

start to V. （105 會考）

stay away from （104 會考）

stay home （104 會考）

stay on top （104 會考）

stop + V-ing （103 會考）

study hard （105 會考）

swoon over （103 會考）

take a bath （104 會考）

take a bus （103 會考）

take a rest （103 會考）

take a test （103 會考）

take a trip （103 會考）

take another road

(105 會考)

take care of (103～105 會考)

take in (104 會考)

take long (105 會考)

take medicine (103 會考)

take orders (105 會考)

take out the garbage

(105 會考)

take photos (105 會考)

take pictures (105 會考)

take *sb*. out (105 會考)

take the first right turn

(103 會考)

take the train (104 會考)

talk about (103～105 會考)

talk on the phone

(105 會考)

talk to *sb*. (103、104 會考)

tell *sb*. about sth.

(105 會考)

thanks for (105 會考)

thanks to (103 會考)

That's too bad (104 會考)

the day after tomorrow

(104 會考)

the day before (105 會考)

the good and bad

(103 會考)

The idea may hit you

(104 會考)

the last N. (103 會考)

the rise and fall (103 會考)

the same way (104 會考)

there + be (103～105 會考)

these days (103、104 會考)

these years (104 會考)

they say (that) (103 會考)

think about (103～105 會考)

think of (104、105 會考)

think of *A* as *B* (104 會考)

this time (103、104 會考) .

those who (104、105 會考)

to start with (104 會考)

together with (103 會考)

too...to V. (104、105 會考)

top five (103 會考)

top place (103 會考)

top ten (103 會考)

touch *one's* heart

(103 會考)

try + V-ing (103 會考)

try hard (103 會考)

try to V. (103～105 會考)

turn back (103、105 會考)

turn into (103 會考)

turn left (105 會考)

turn off (103、105 會考)

turn out (104 會考)

under the ground

(105 會考)

up there (104 會考)

use *one's* time well

(104 會考)

use the bathroom

(104 會考)

use up (103 會考)

used to V. (103～105 會考)

very much (103 會考)

wait and see (104 會考)

wait for (104、105 會考)

wake *sb*. up (103 會考)

wake up (104 會考)

walk around (104 會考)

walk out of (105 會考)

walk past (103 會考)

want to V. (104、105 會考)

warm up (104 會考)

warmer and warmer

(104 會考)

What a small world!

(104 會考)

What do you mean by...?

(103 會考)

What do you say?

(103 會考)

What do you think

about...? (105 會考)

what is worse (104 會考)

what's more (104 會考)

What's wrong with...?

(105 會考)

whether...or not (105 會考)

Why not? (103 會考)

win *one's* heart back

(104 會考)

work as (105 會考)

work on (103 會考)

worry about (104 會考)

would like to V. (103～105

會考)

write down (104、105 會考)

you know (103 會考)

you never know

(105 會考)

劉毅英文國中部同學獎學金排行榜

姓　名	就讀學校	總金額	姓　名	就讀學校	總金額	姓　名	就讀學校	總金額
邱浩瑋	麗山國中	15000	郭辰安	仁愛國中	8000	黃柏叡	內湖國中	6000
曹紘瀠	士林國中	11000	葉忠諺	復興國中	8000	楊佑翎	民生國中	6000
呂沄諮	敦化國中	11000	闕湘庭	成淵國中	8000	賴識涵	積穗國小	6000
顧存困	碧華國中	10000	陳柏憲	市三民國中	8000	林偉宏	永平國中	6000
羅仕杰	士林國中	10000	吳慶麟	市明德國中	8000	許靜雯	大安國中	6000
陳彥龍	景興國中	10000	石沛潔	衛理女中	8000	王靜慧	太平國小	6000
劉煌基	懷生國中	10000	楊詠舜	政大附中國中部	8000	郭思廷	明湖國中	6000
郭子靖	麗山國中	10000	丁紀元	市中正國中	8000	陳宥云	靜心國小	6000
陳均愷	龍門國中	10000	曾亭諺	天母國中	8000	林玄雅	介壽國中	6000
許煥承	積穗國中	10000	邱昶元	龍門國中	8000	吳晏儀	東湖國小	6000
簡婕翎	立人國中	10000	陳怡雯	薇閣高中	8000	盧證皓	景興國中	6000
蔡佳頤	仁愛國中	10000	賴靜文	蘭雅國中	8000	林正浩	縣中正國中	6000
游一心	銘傳國中	10000	許珈瑜	萬華國中	8000	卓庭仔	東湖國中	6000
周士捷	福和國中	9400	陸冠霖	光仁國中	7000	游敦智	實踐國中	6000
葉紹傑	復旦國中	9000	王林智	金華國中	7000	洪菀君	及人中學	6000
廖珮妤	延平國中部	9000	高瑄吟	北安國中	7000	陳明洋	和平國中	6000
陳　沖	天母國中	9000	劉易奇	仁愛國中	7000	陳筱翎	積穗國中	6000
李健柔	華興國中	9000	呂姿穎	錦和高中	7000	薛昭慈	丹鳳國中	6000
沈禹佑	介壽國中	9000	黃泓翔	三和國中	7000	陳俐霖	市中山國中	6000
劉冠伶	弘道國中	9000	黃品勛	福和國中	7000	顏鳳而	中道國中	6000
江柏葳	市中山國中	9000	郭謹豪	大安國中	7000	郭玟伶	市明德國中	6000
李姵蓁	中平國中	9000	陳詠恩	介壽國中	7000	吳晨瑜	徐匯國中	5000
潘奕勳	慧燈國中	9000	張羽昊	麗山國中	7000	徐紫媛	古亭國中	3550
陳咸安	麗山國中	9000	賴揚軒	碧華國中	7000	韋子中	成淵國中	3000
丁初寧	仁愛國中	9000	蕭　愃	百齡國中	7000	游欣頻	師大附中國中部	2000
簡彣熹	明湖國中	9000	劉達元	萬芳國中	7000	鄭惠心	明湖國中	2000
許雯涵	華興國中	9000	郭柏成	蘆洲國中	7000	張曉晴	大安國中	1000
林子馨	南門國中	9000	徐柏翰	誠正國中	7000	曹瀞文	百齡國中	1000
黃巧慧	東山國中	9000	江美吟	光榮國中	7000	李浩羽	海山國中	1000
李曜宇	建成國中	9000	吳維緒	麗山國中	7000	許雅筑	萬芳國中	1000
蘇知適	成淵國中	9000	林怡安	市中正國中	6000	黃品瑄	金陵女中	1000
林佳璇	薇格國中部	8000	康紘瑋	錦和國中	6000	王品淳	衛理女中	1000
梁恩綺	仁愛國中	8000	陳奕愷	仁愛國中	6000			

劉毅英文教育機構

台北市許昌街17號6F（捷運M8出口對面・學善補習班）　　　TEL：（02）2389-5212
台中市三民路三段125號7F（光南文具批發樓上・劉毅補習班）　TEL：（04）2221-8861

<附錄>

學習出版公司優良學生獎學金申請辦法

　　凡是國三同學學校模擬考試，任何一次英文分數，得到班上前 5 名，可得「學習出版公司」圖書禮券 500 元。台北地區同學，請持本表，親至「台北市許昌街 17 號 6 F」（壽德大樓）領取。【週一至週五下午 4：00 ～ 9：00，週六、週日上午 8：30 ～ 下午 6：00】

　　台北地區以外的同學，請將本表寄至「學習出版公司」，並註明 500 元等值之書籍。【請於成績公佈後，一週內申請，逾期以棄權論，每人限領一次。】

學習出版公司優良學生獎學金申請表

姓　　名	
就讀學校	班　級
電　　話	
地　　址	

國三第 _____ 次模考英文分數 _____ 分，全班第 _____ 名

英文老師 姓　　名	
地　　址	
電　　話	
簽　　章	

◆ 請寄至：台北市大安區 106 敦化南路二段 63 巷 65 號 3F 之 1

歷屆國中會考英文試題全集【珍藏版】

主　　　編 / 劉　毅

發　行　所 / 學習出版有限公司　　　☎ (02) 2704-5525

郵 撥 帳 號 / 05127272 學習出版社帳戶

登　記　證 / 局版台業 2179 號

印　刷　所 / 裕強彩色印刷有限公司

台 北 門 市 / 台北市許昌街 10 號 2 F　　☎ (02) 2331-4060

台灣總經銷 / 紅螞蟻圖書有限公司　　　☎ (02) 2795-3656

本公司網址　www.learnbook.com.tw

電 子 郵 件　learnbook@learnbook.com.tw

售價：新台幣二百二十元正

2016 年 6 月 1 日初版